I0491624

Halloween
Coloring Book

Adult Coloring Books

Aryla Publishing 2017

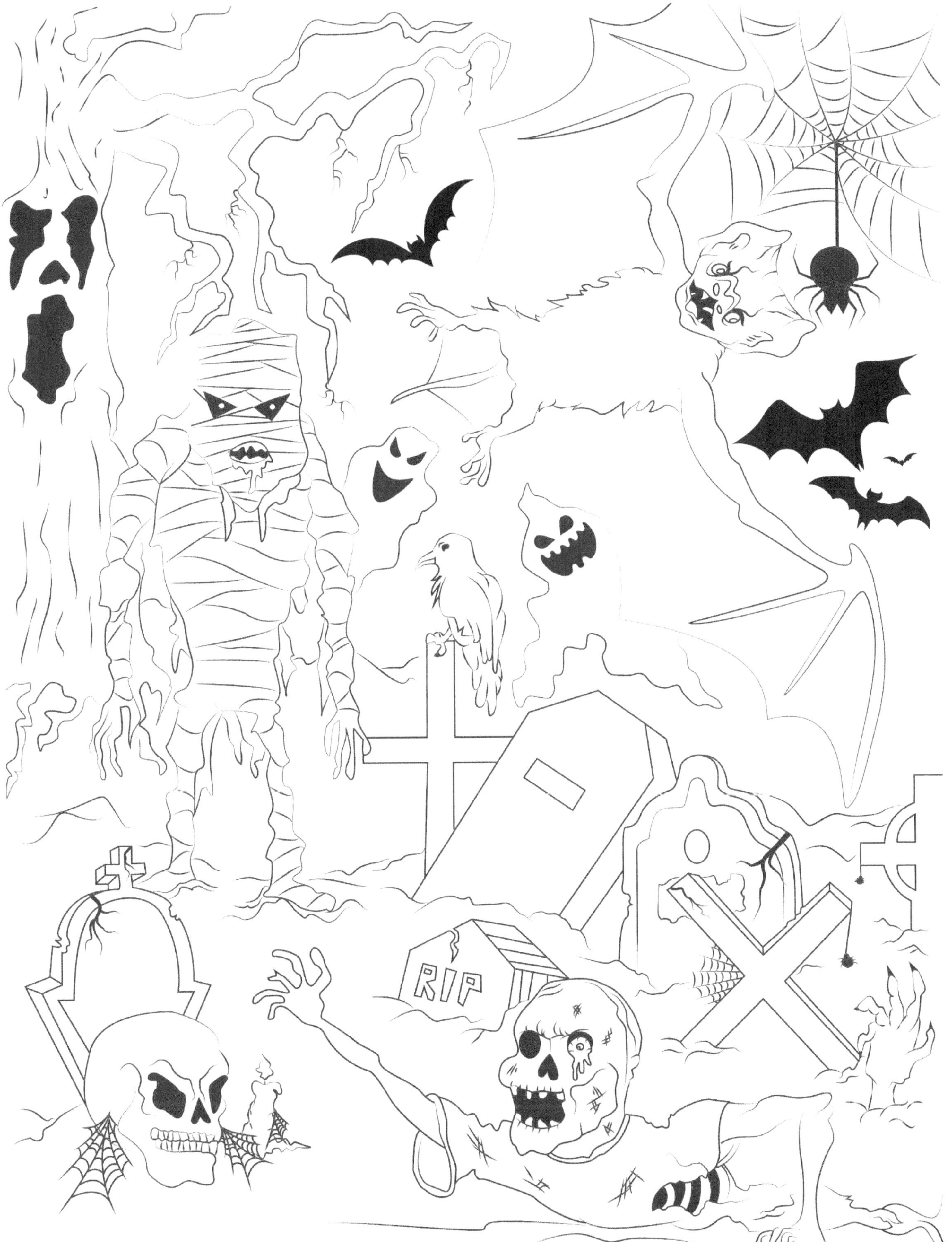
RIP

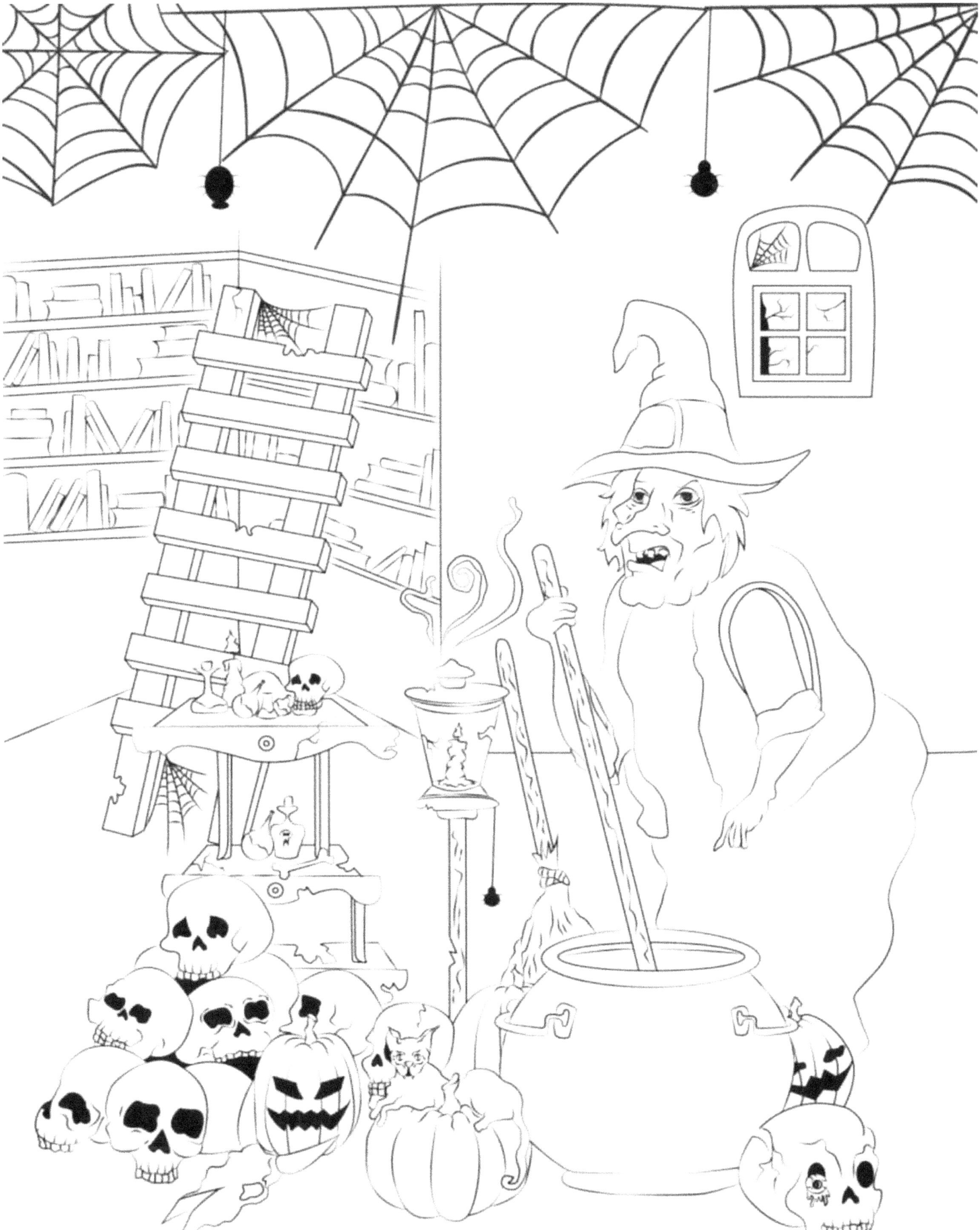

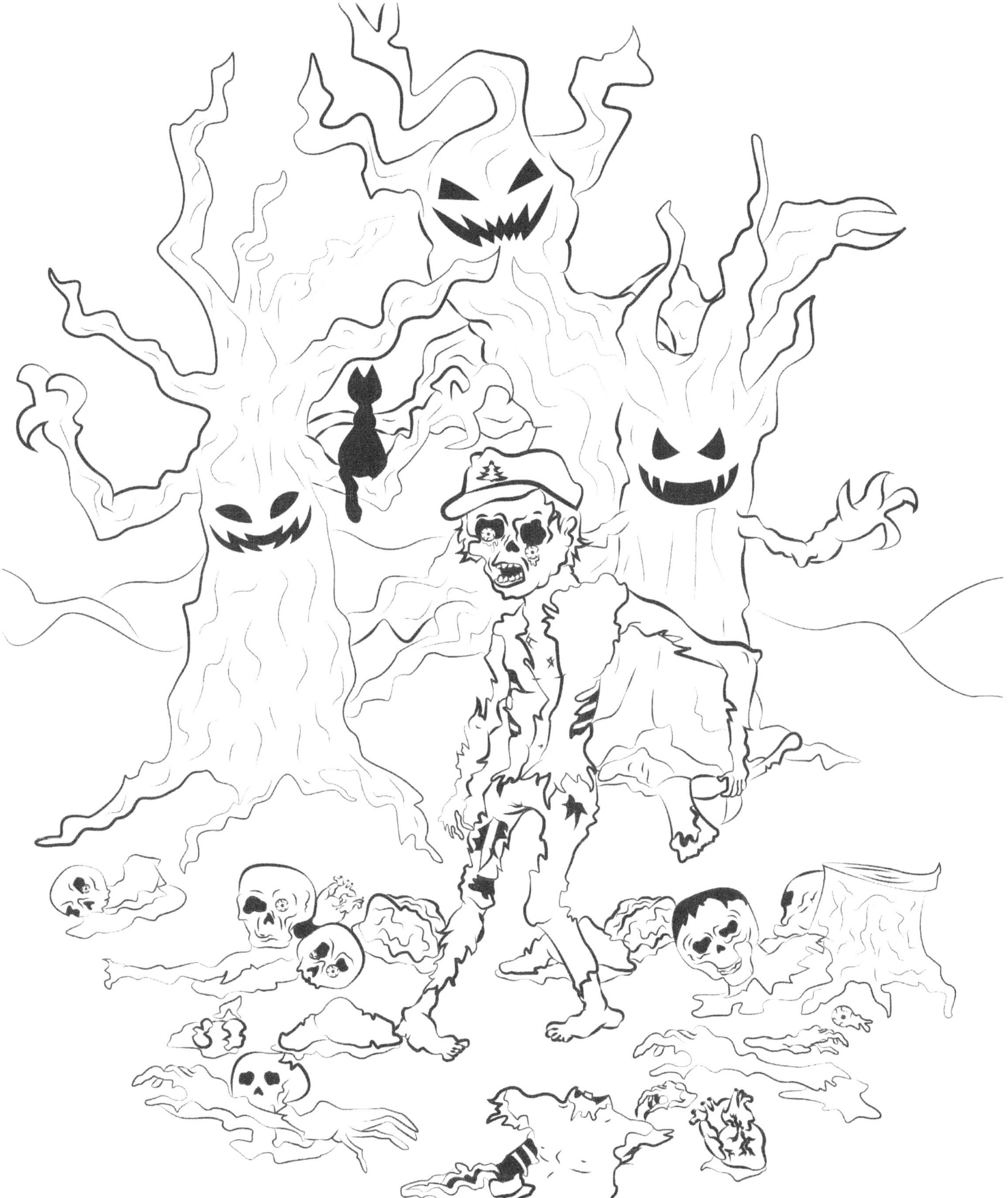

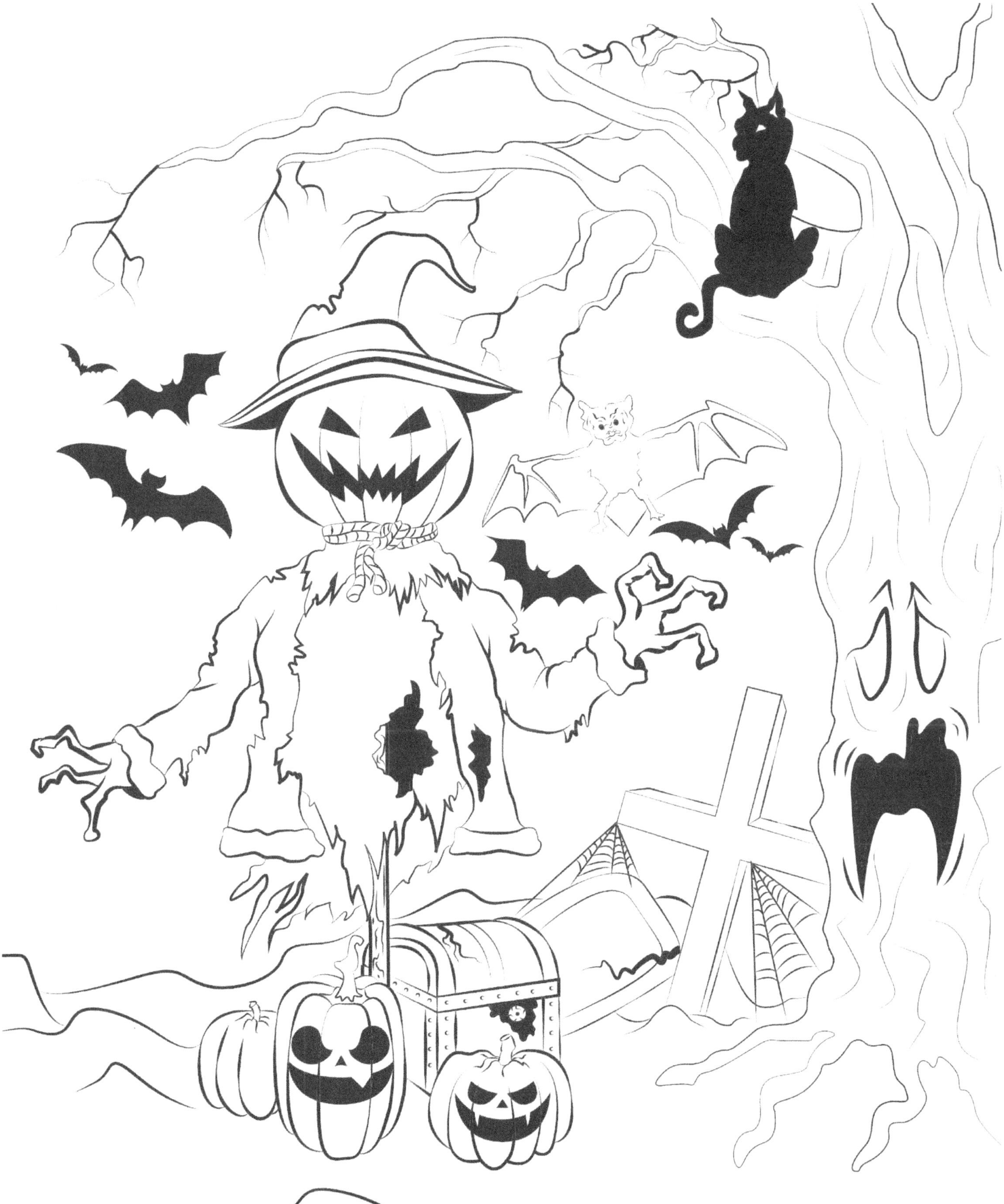

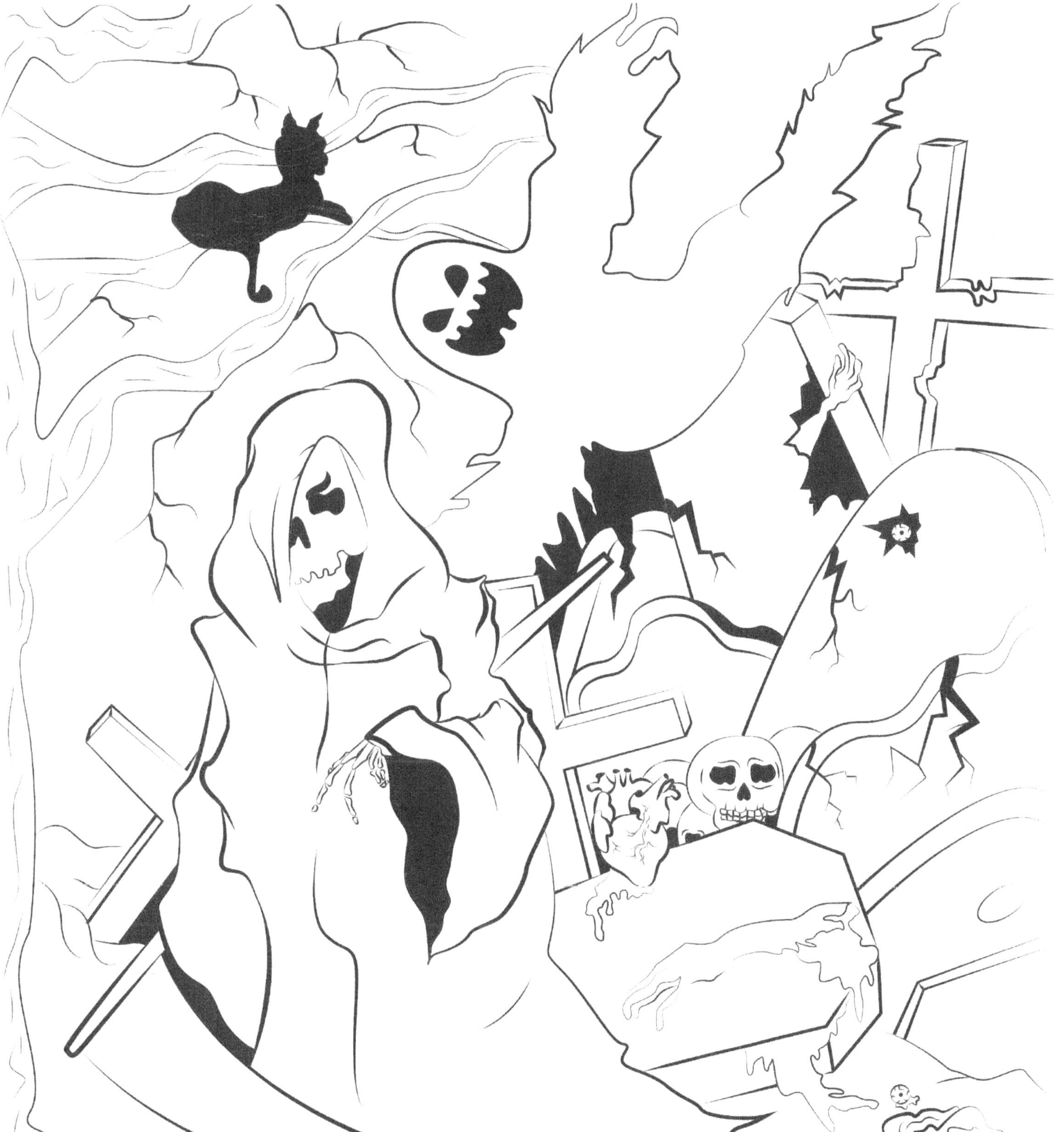

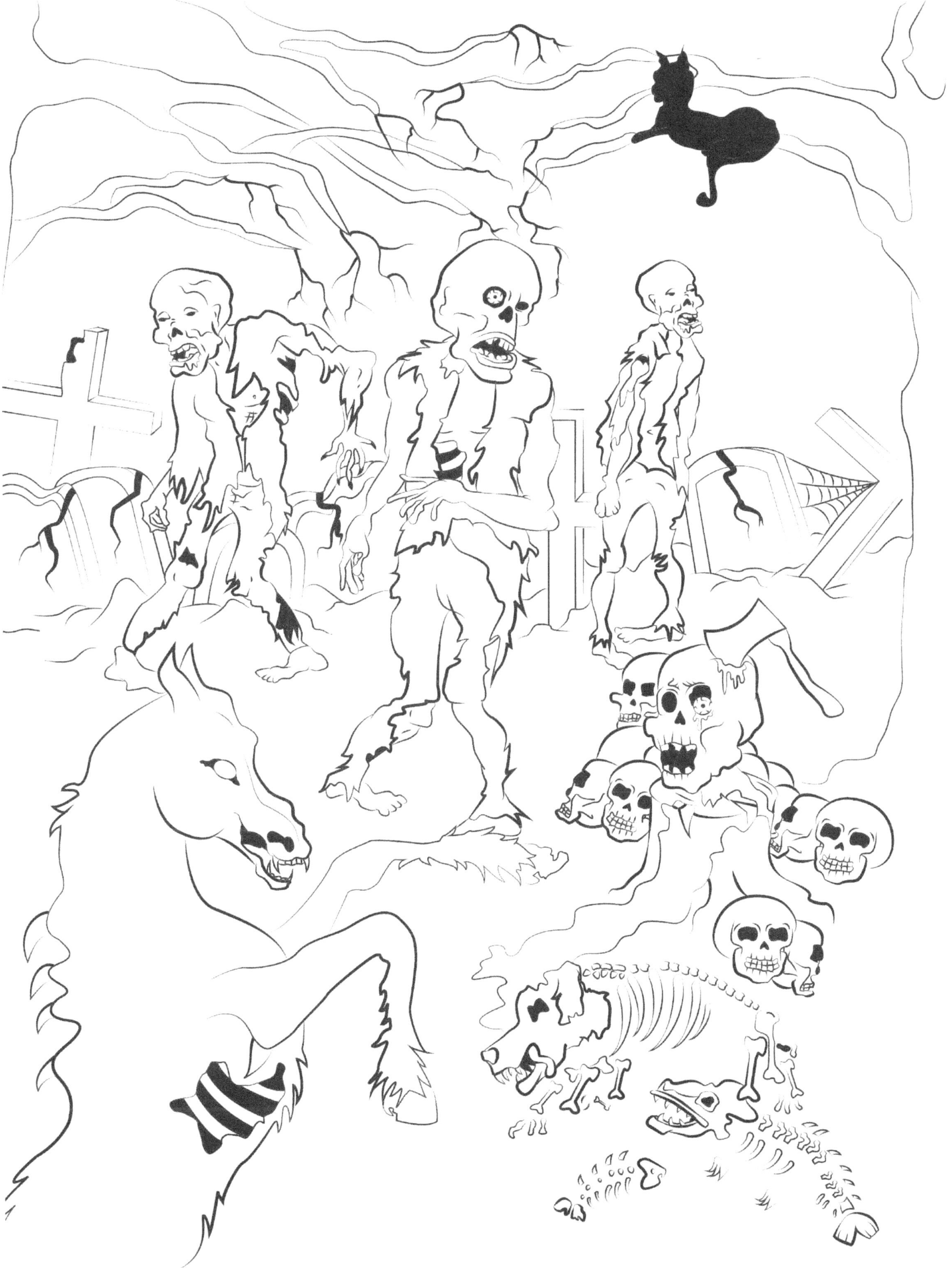

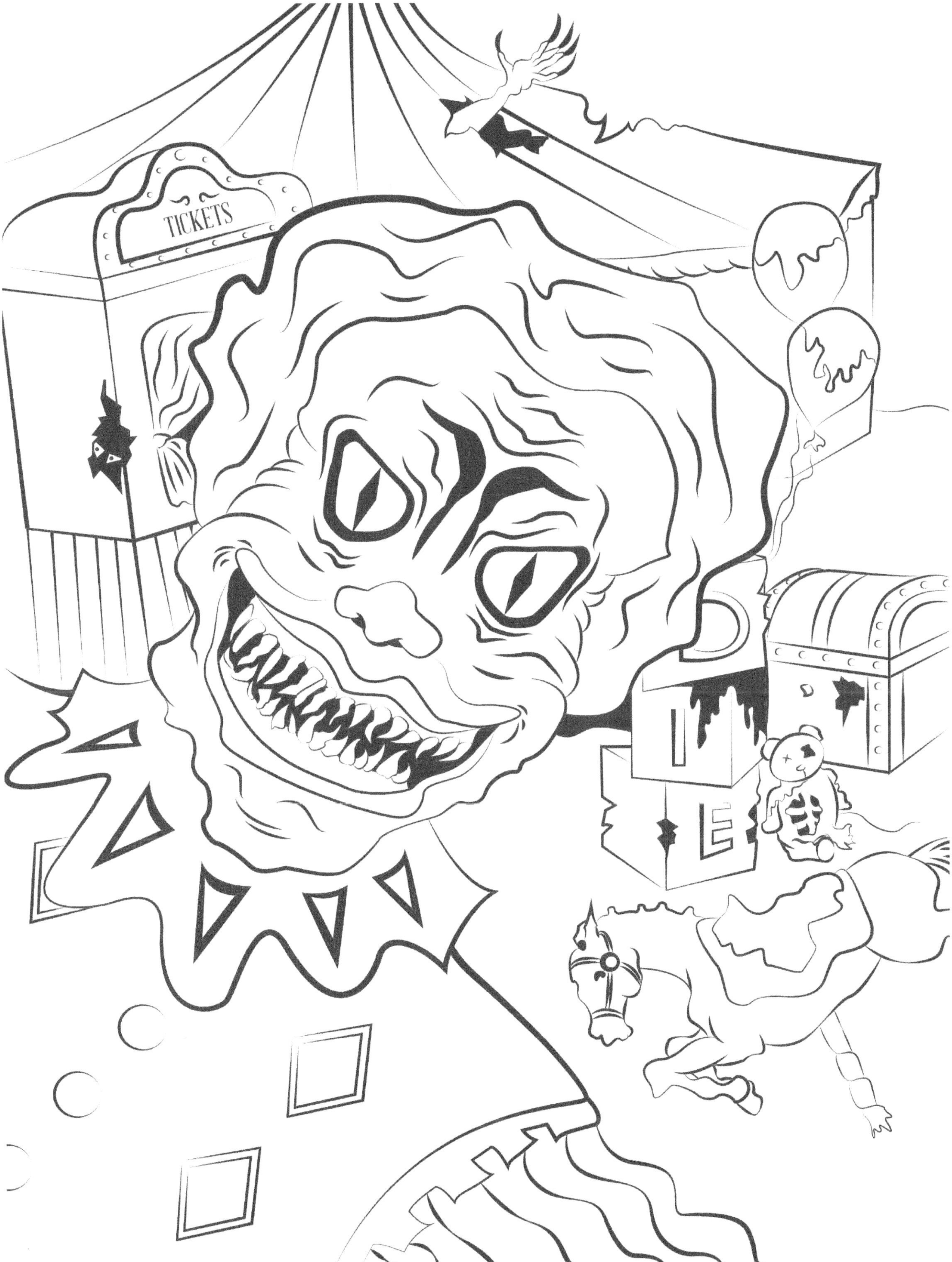
TICKETS

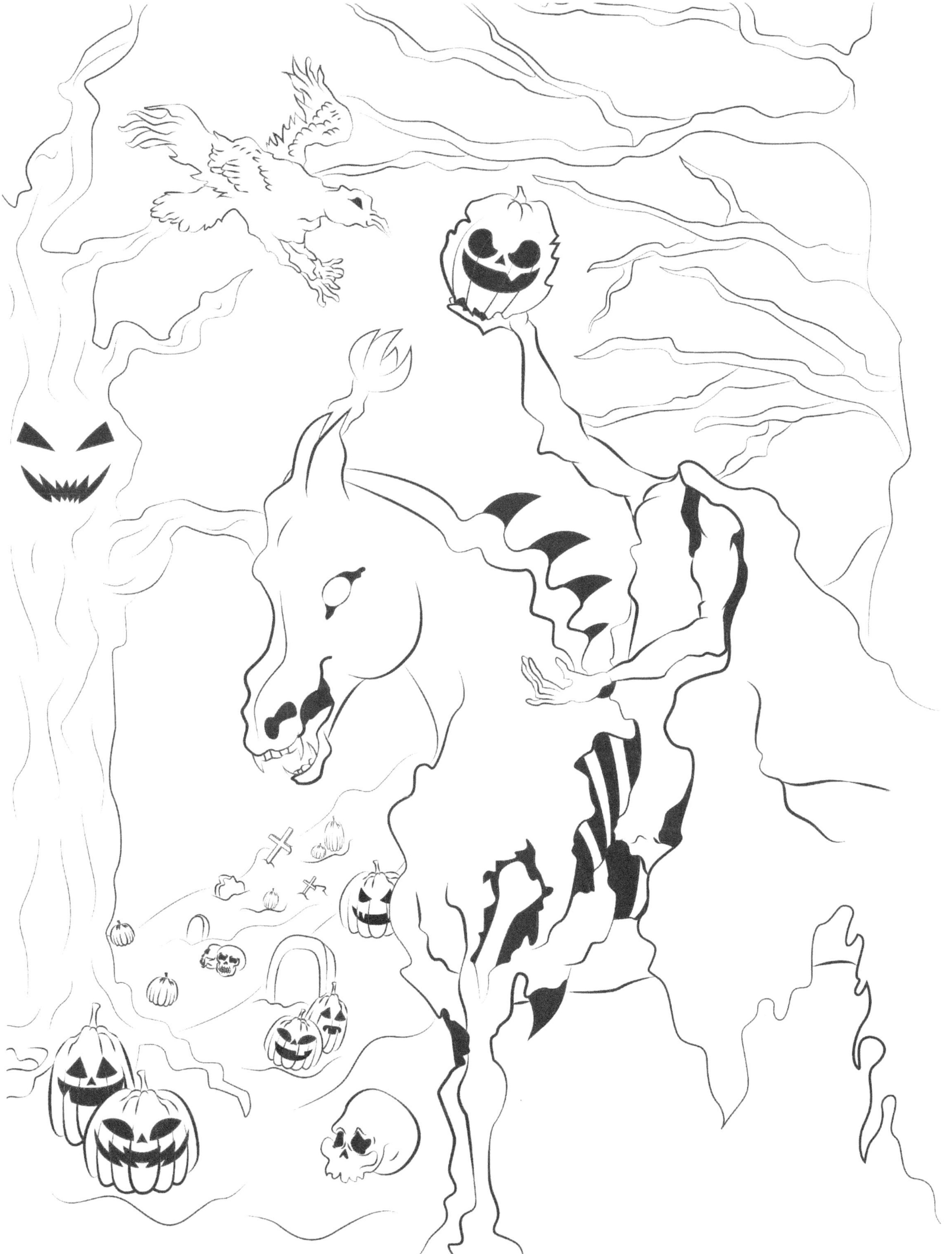

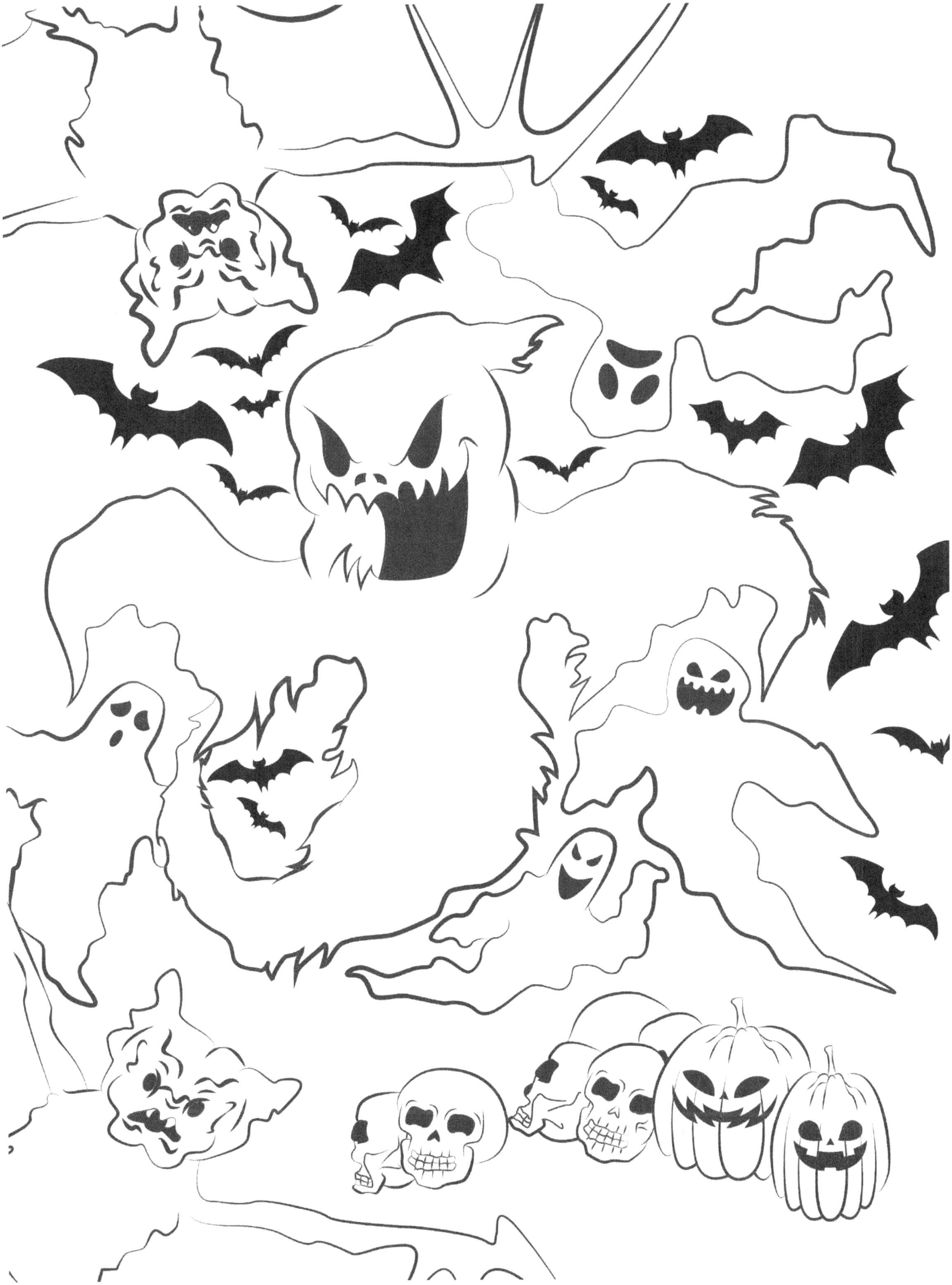

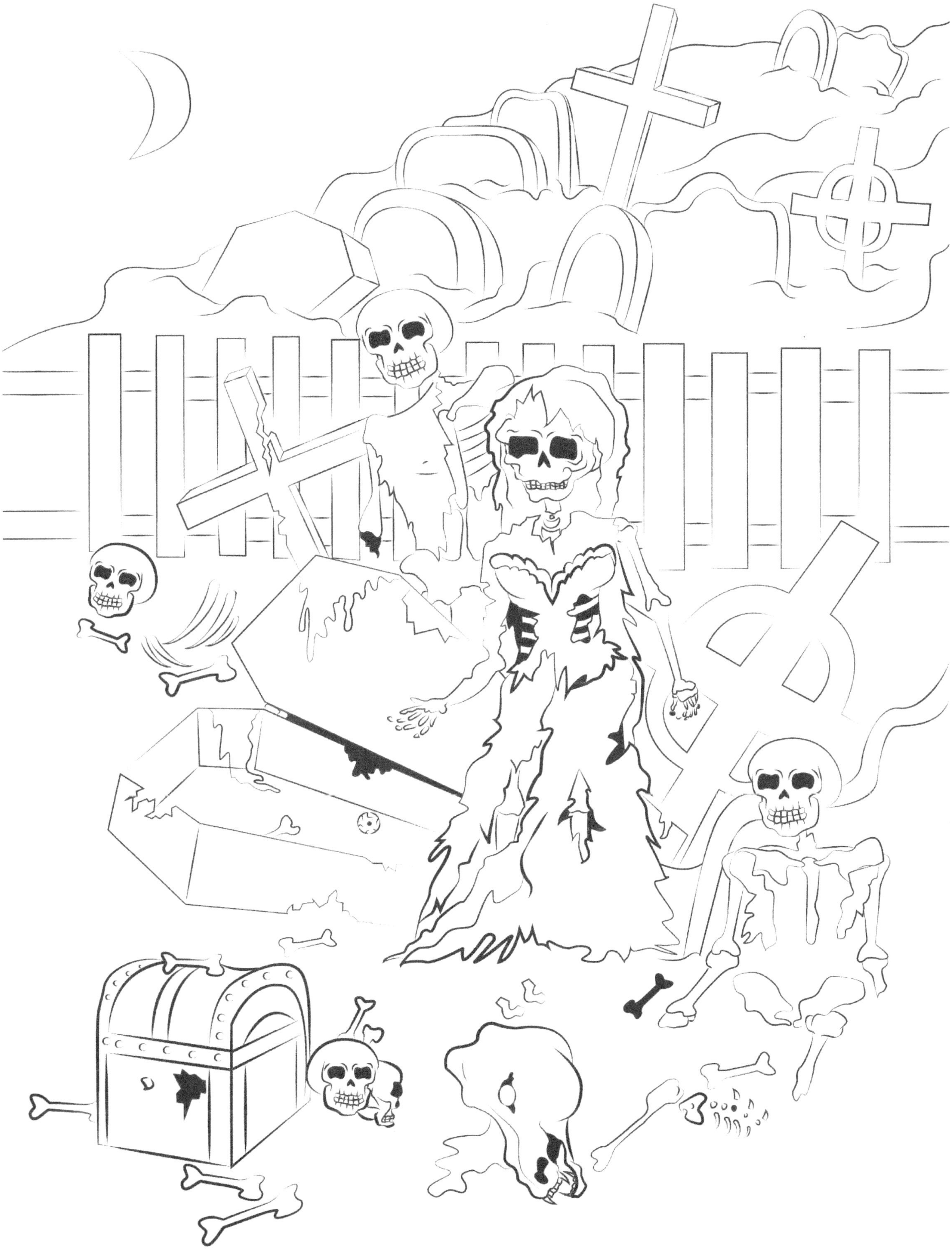

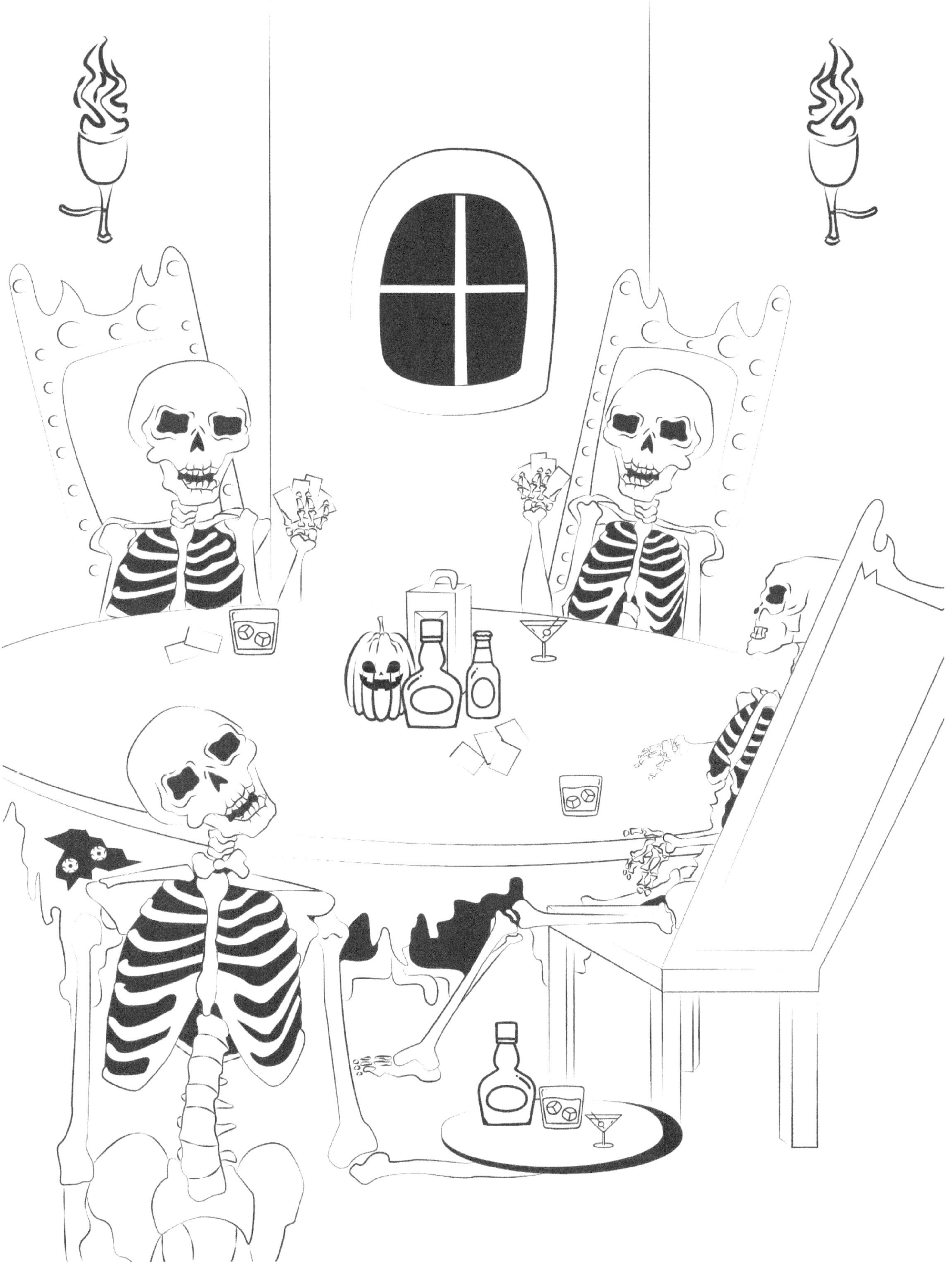

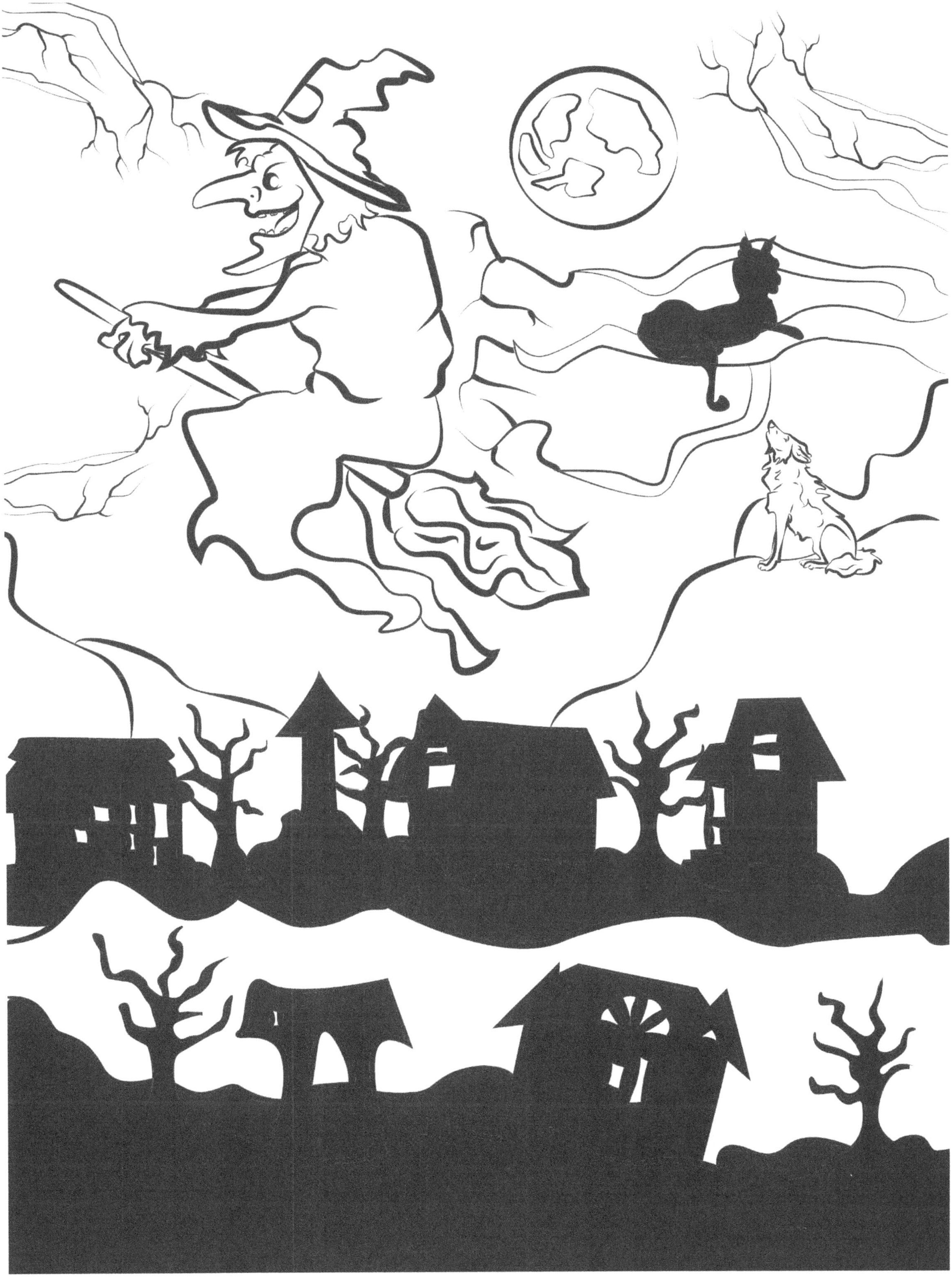

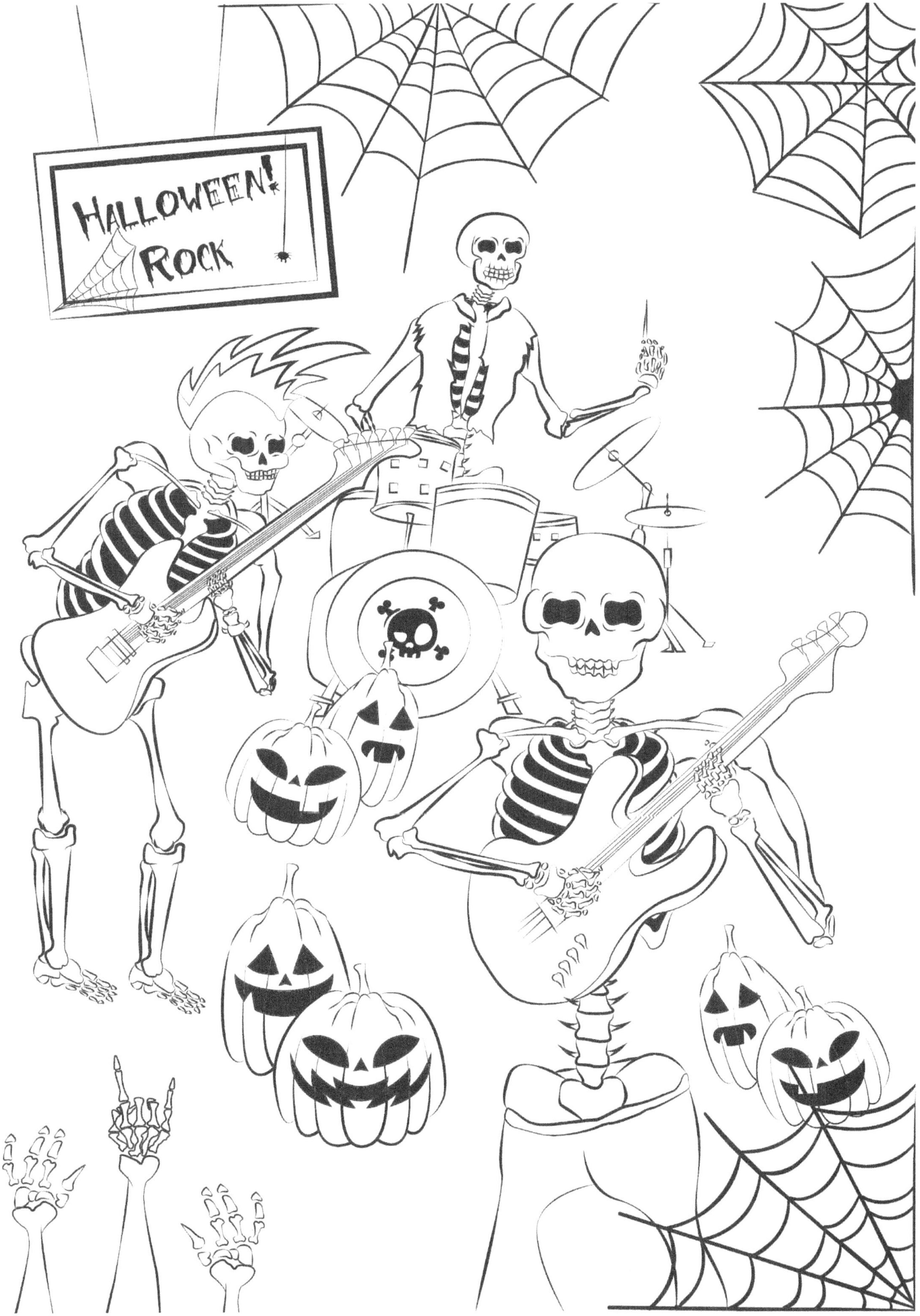
HALLOWEEN!
ROCK

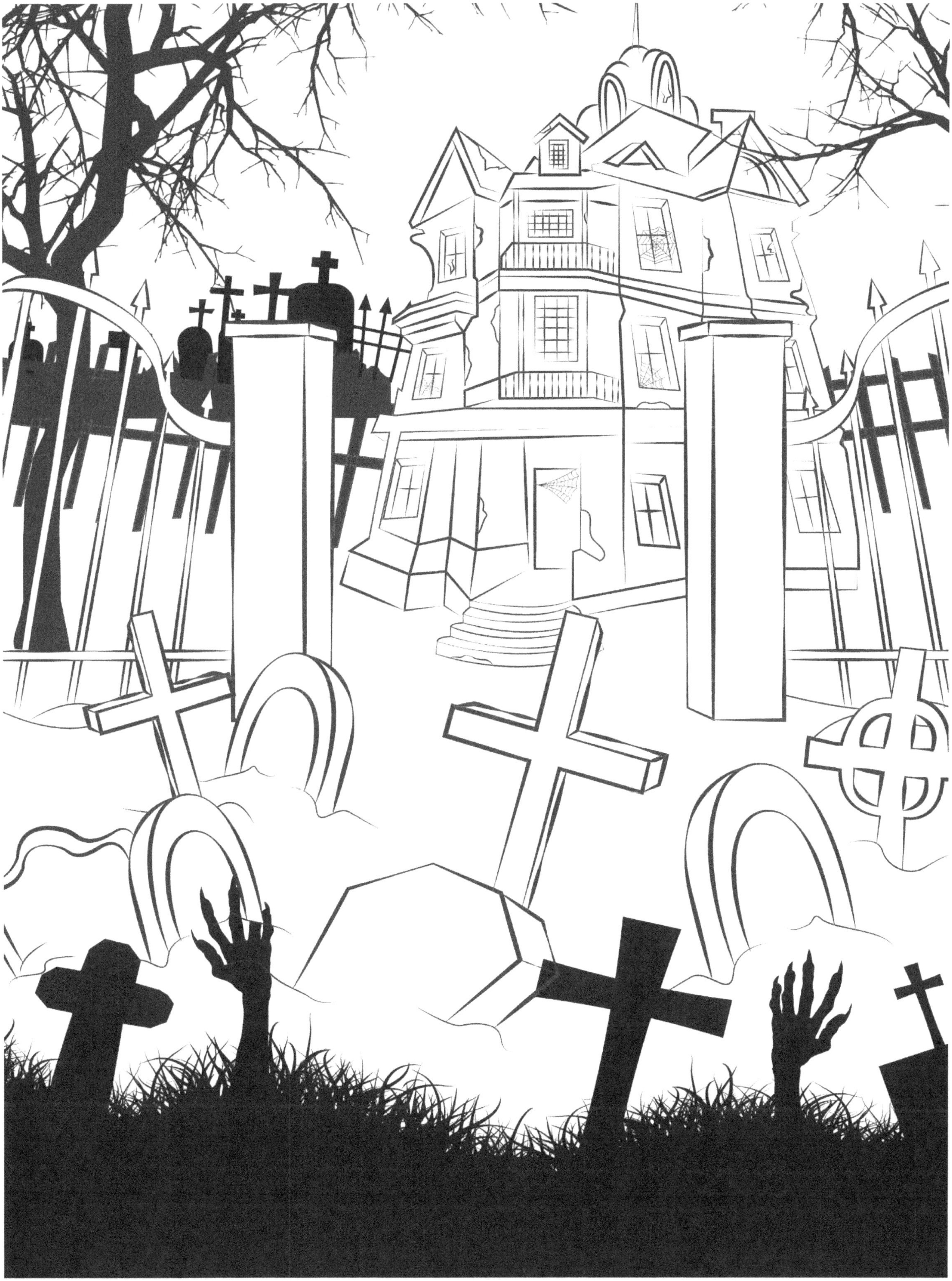

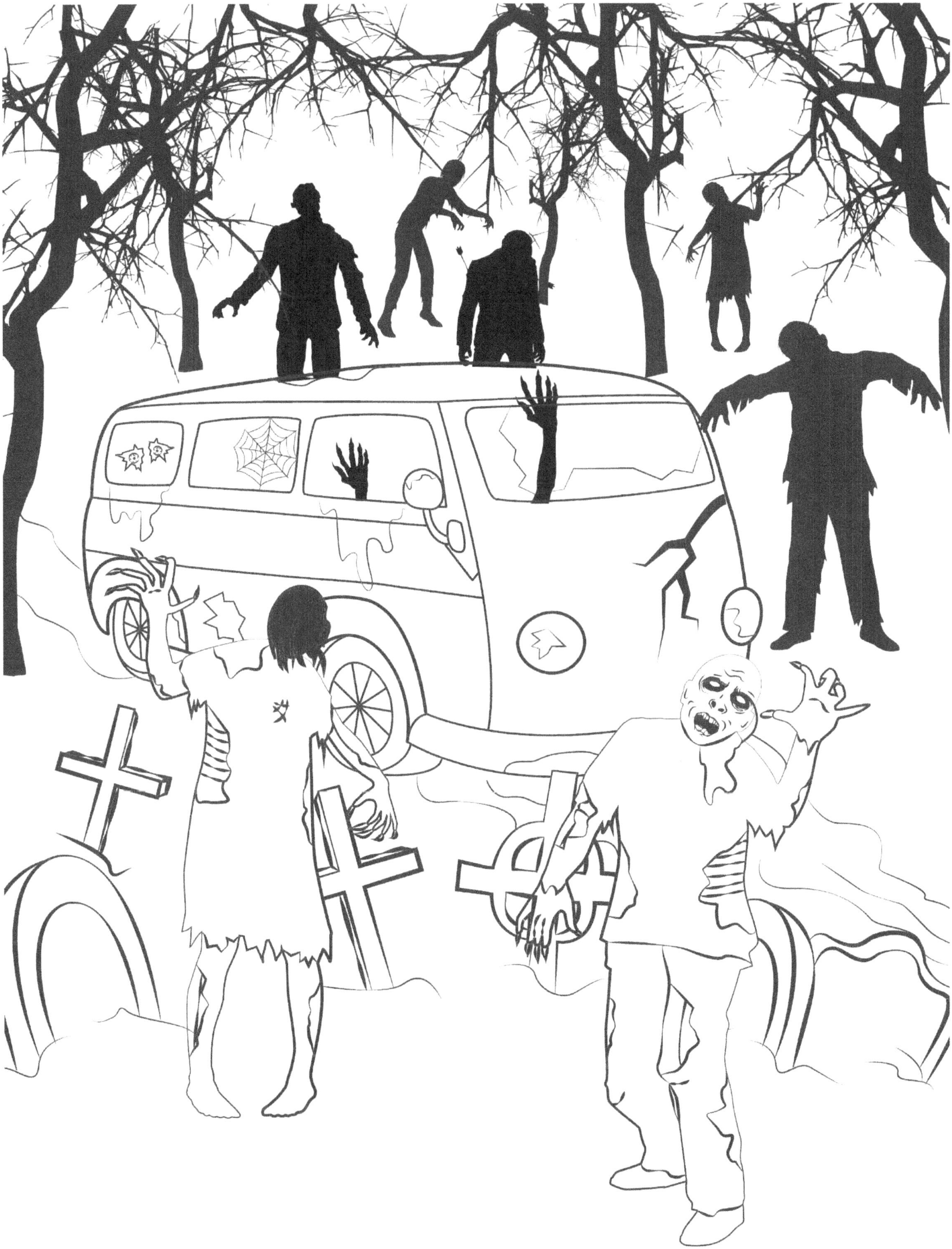

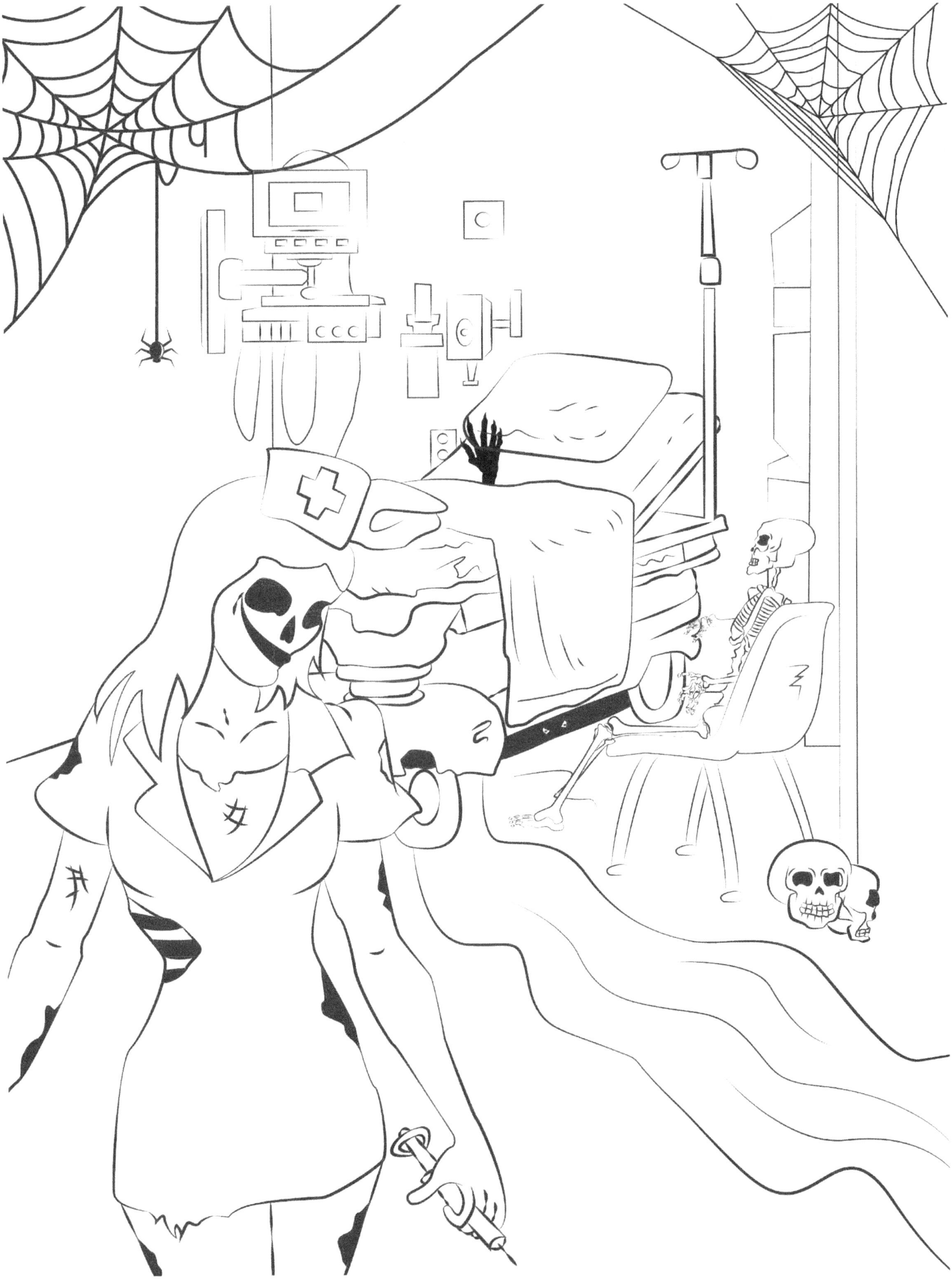

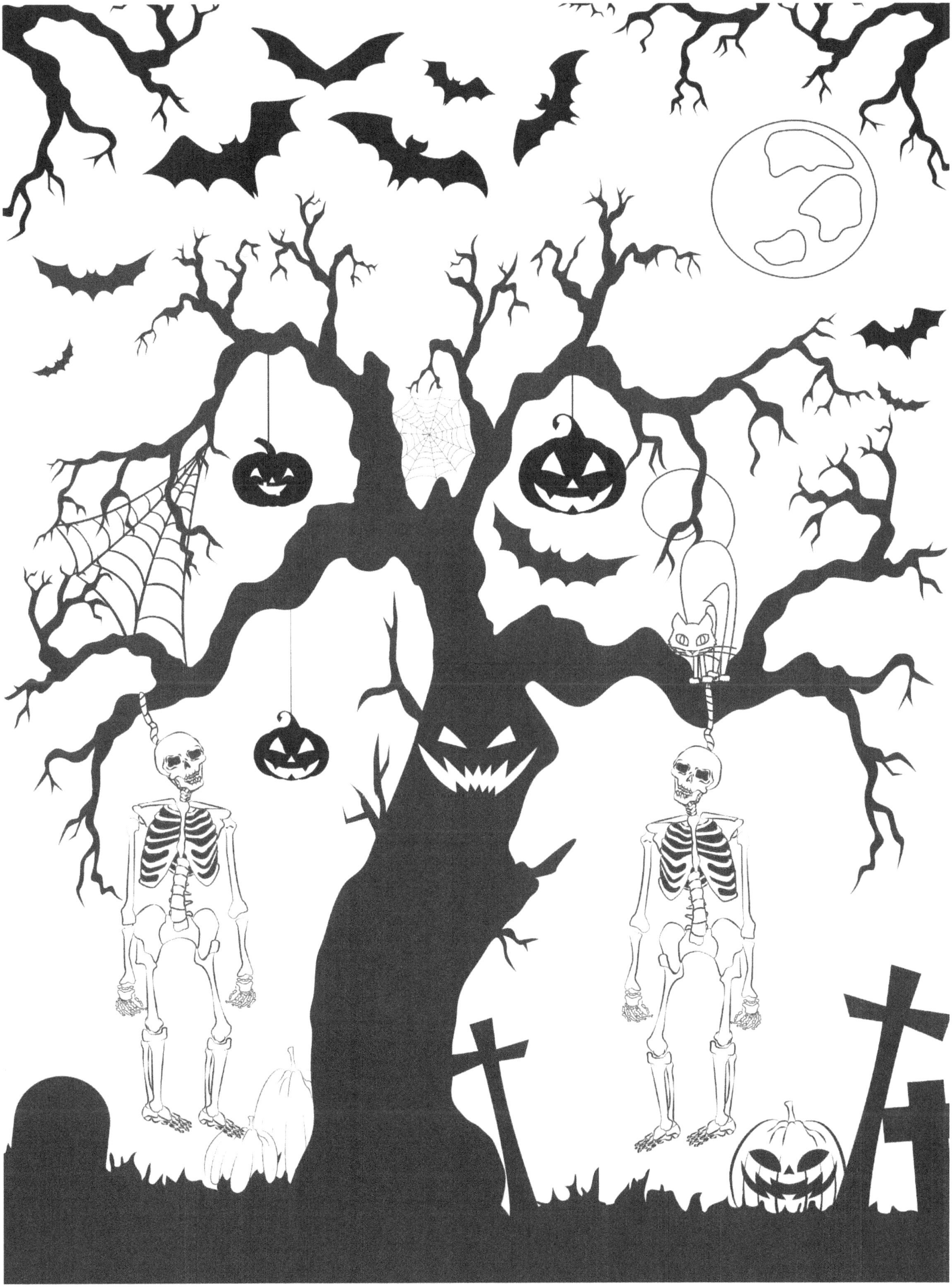

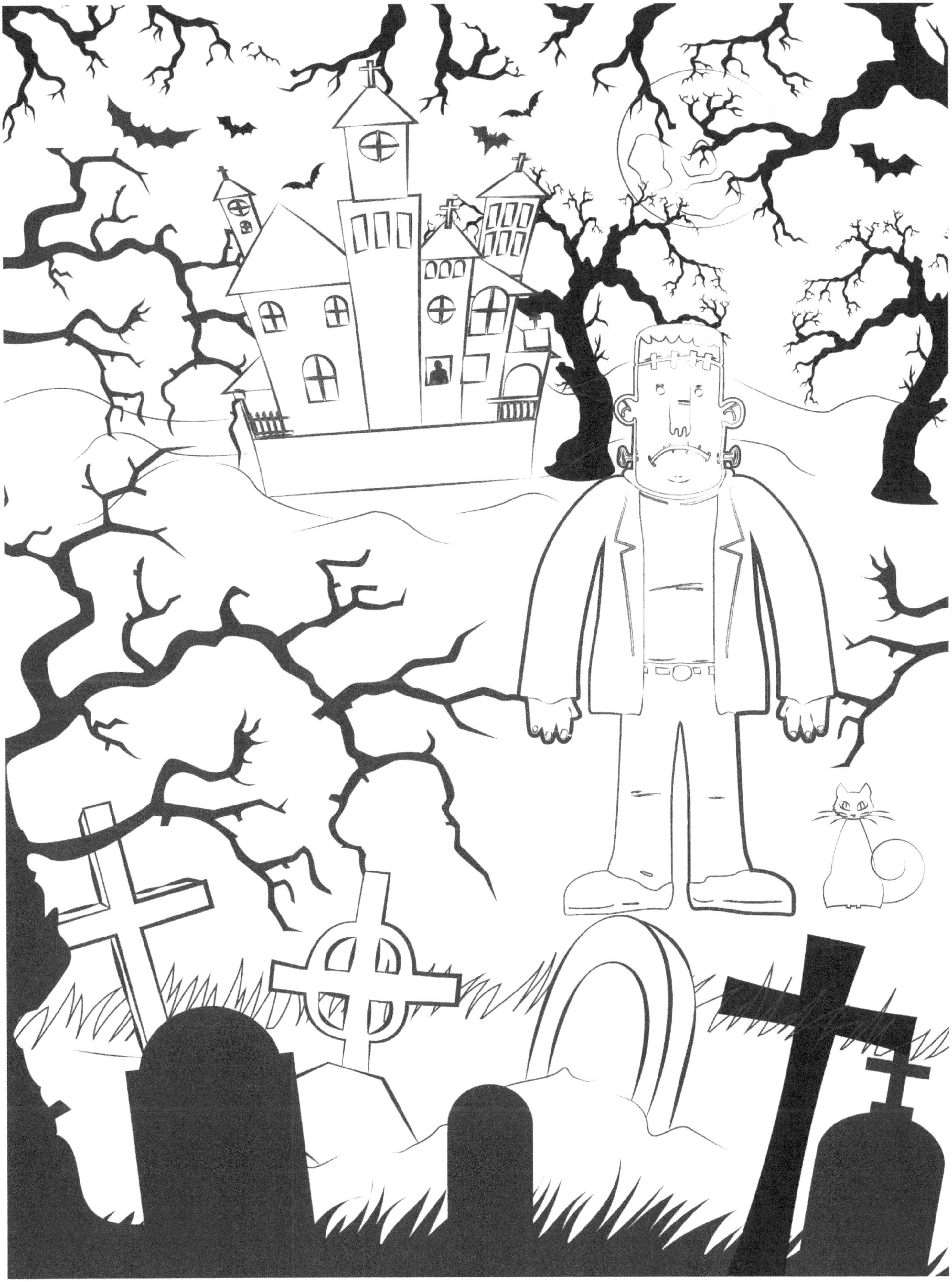

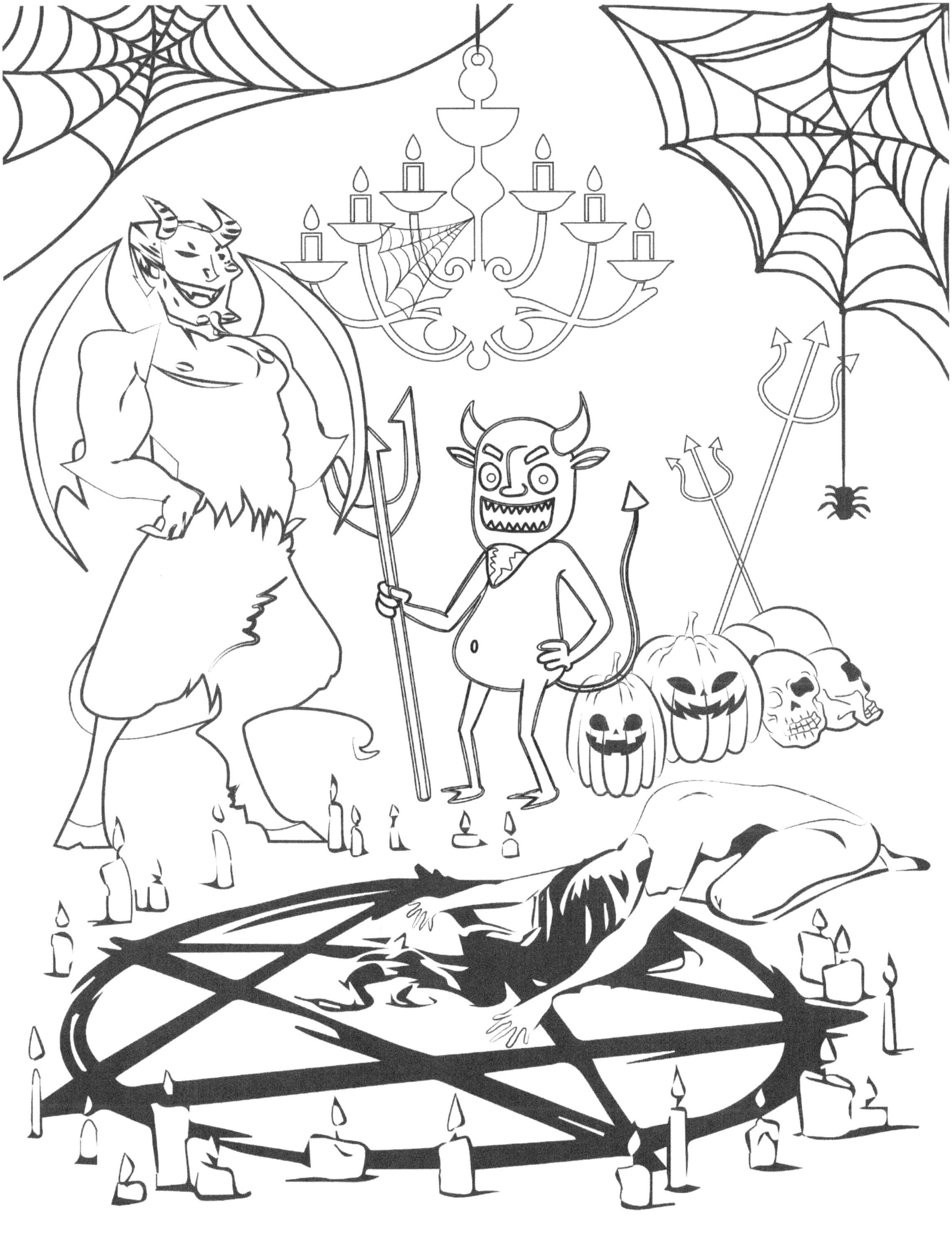

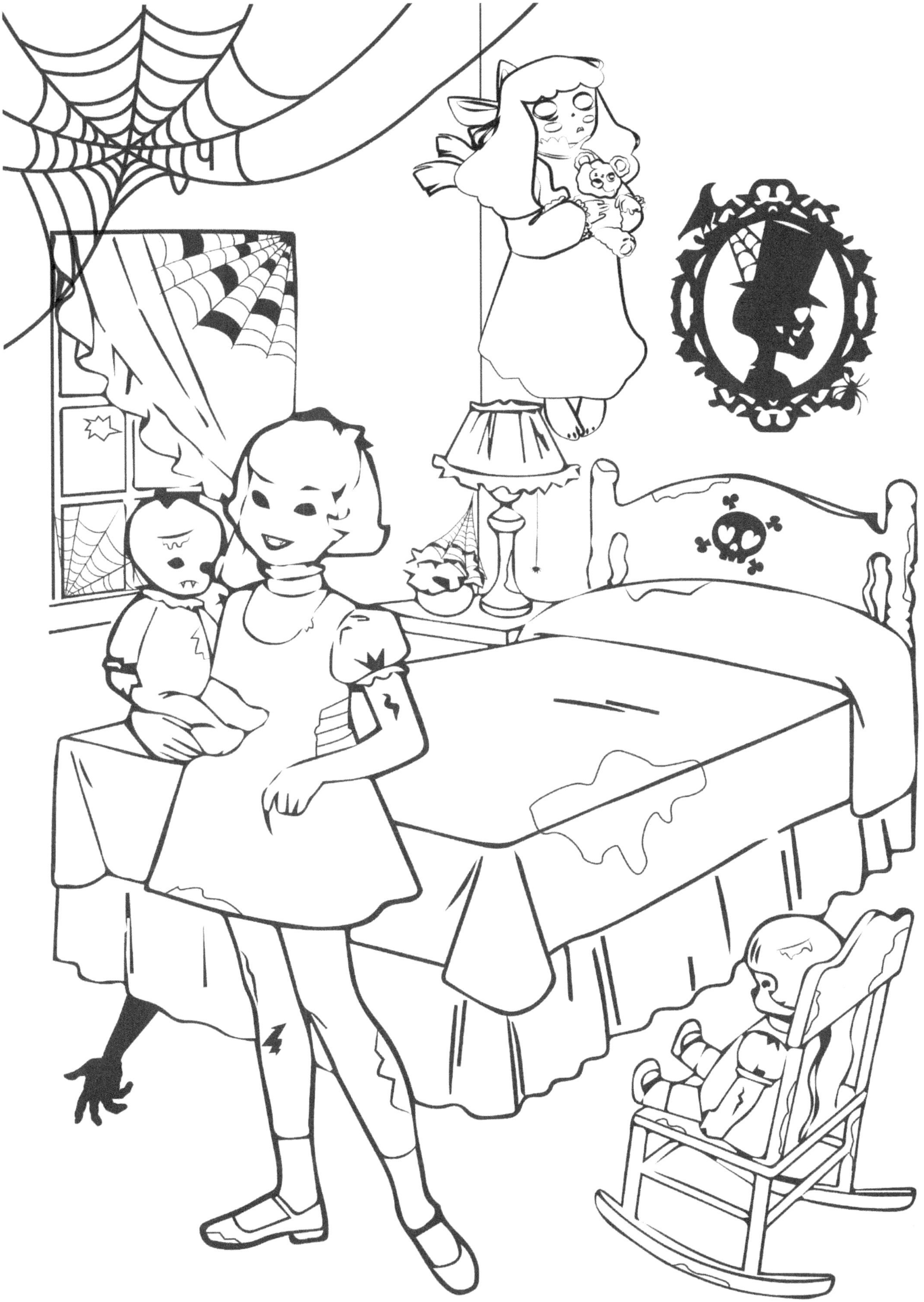

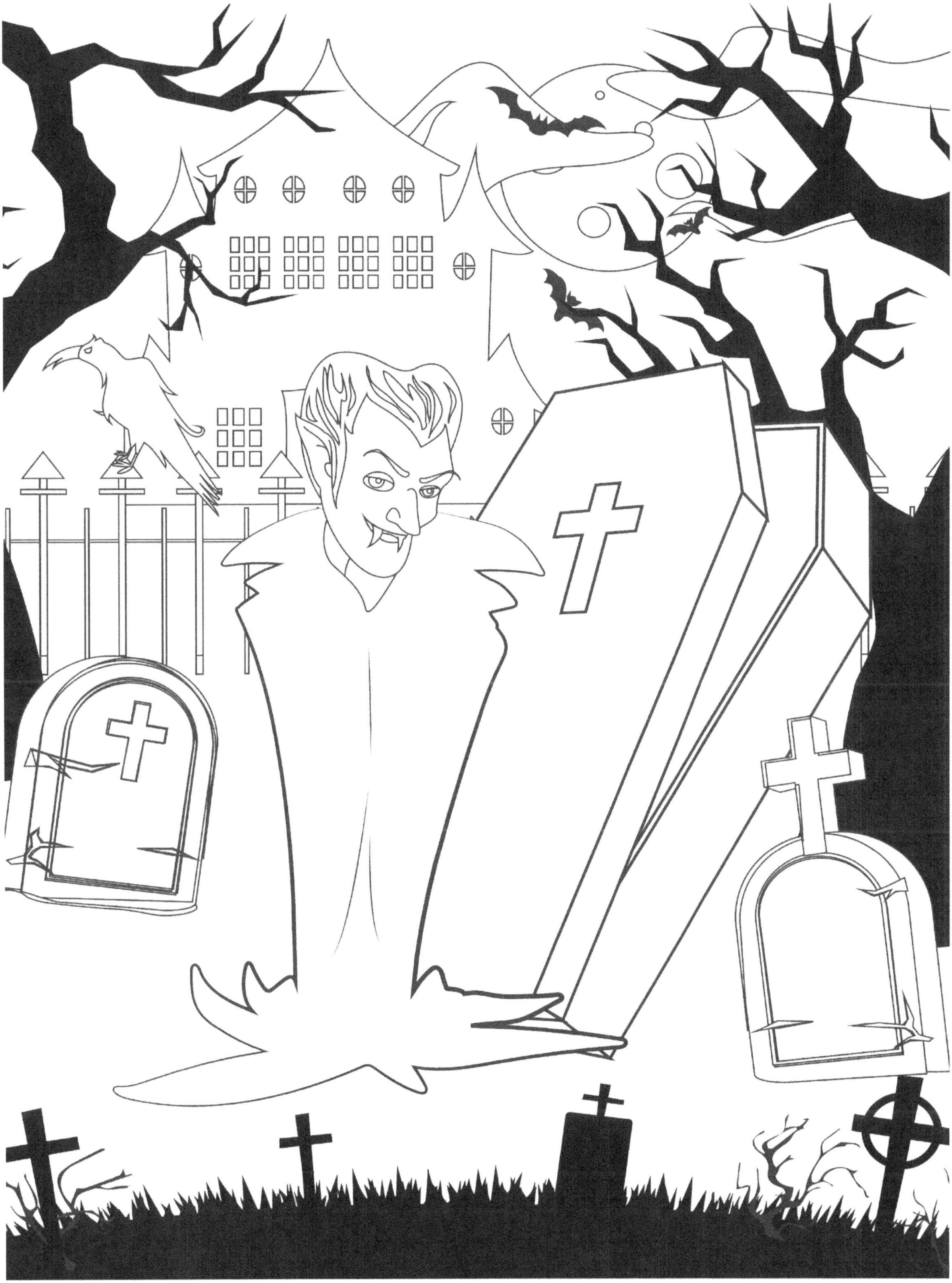

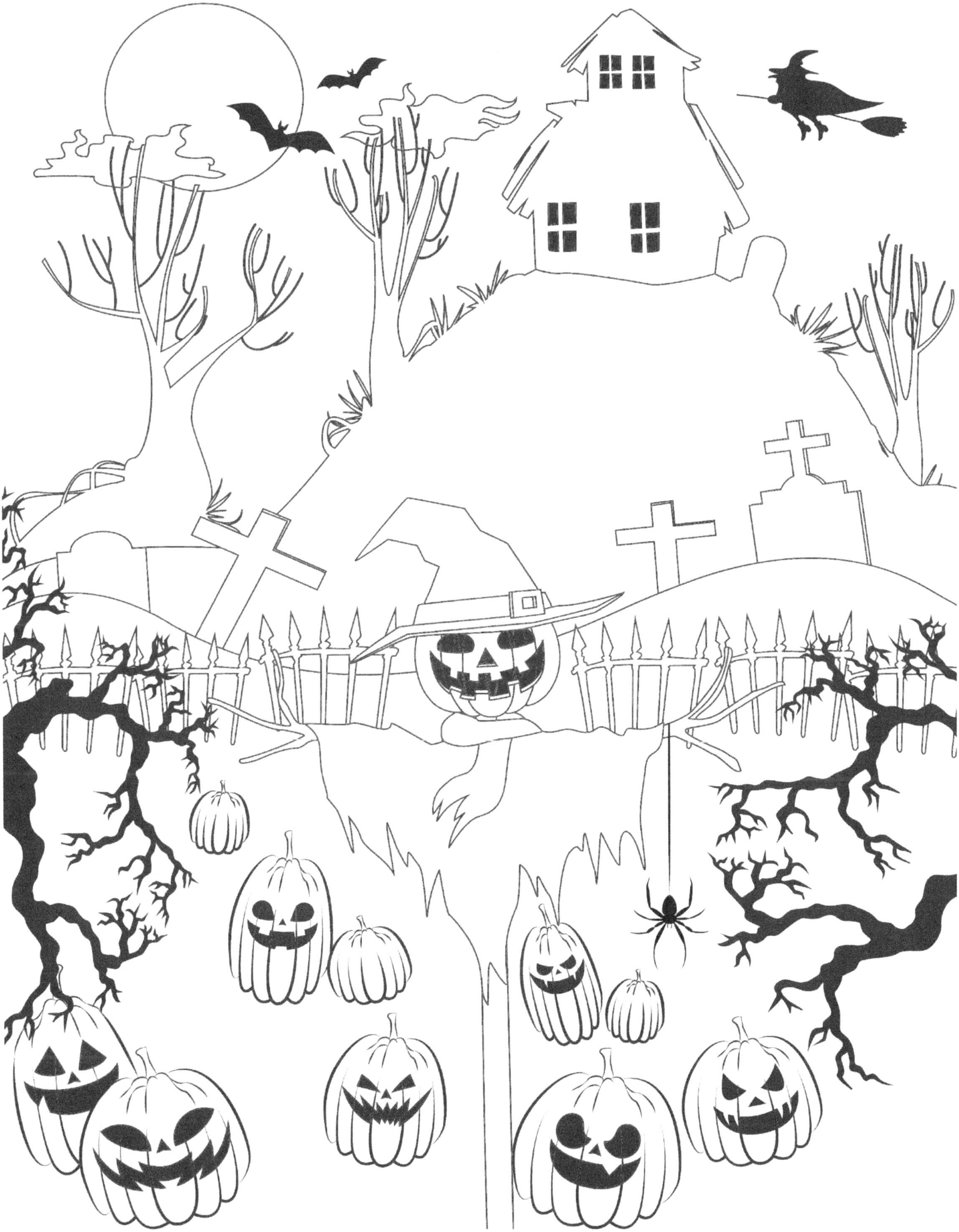

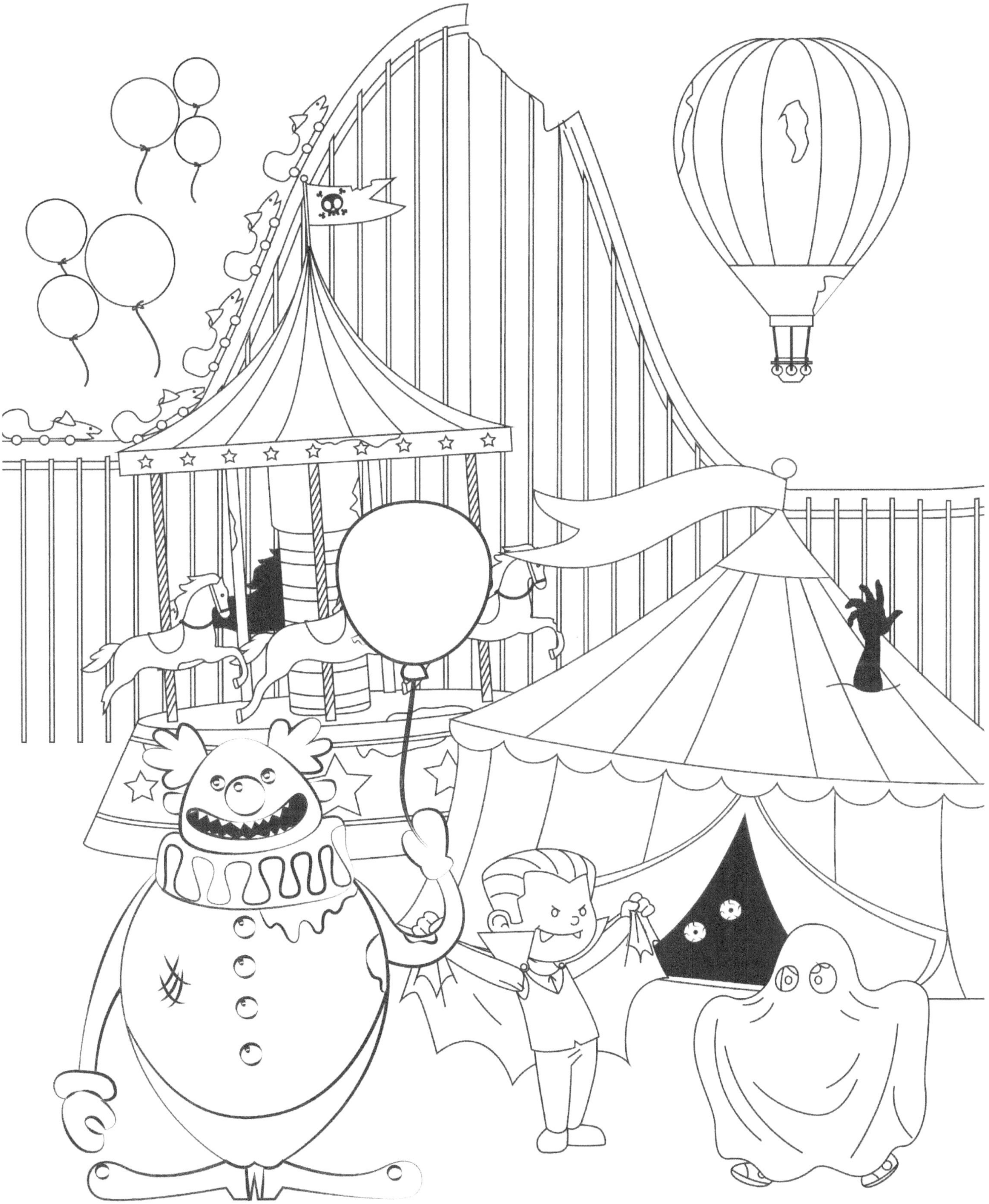

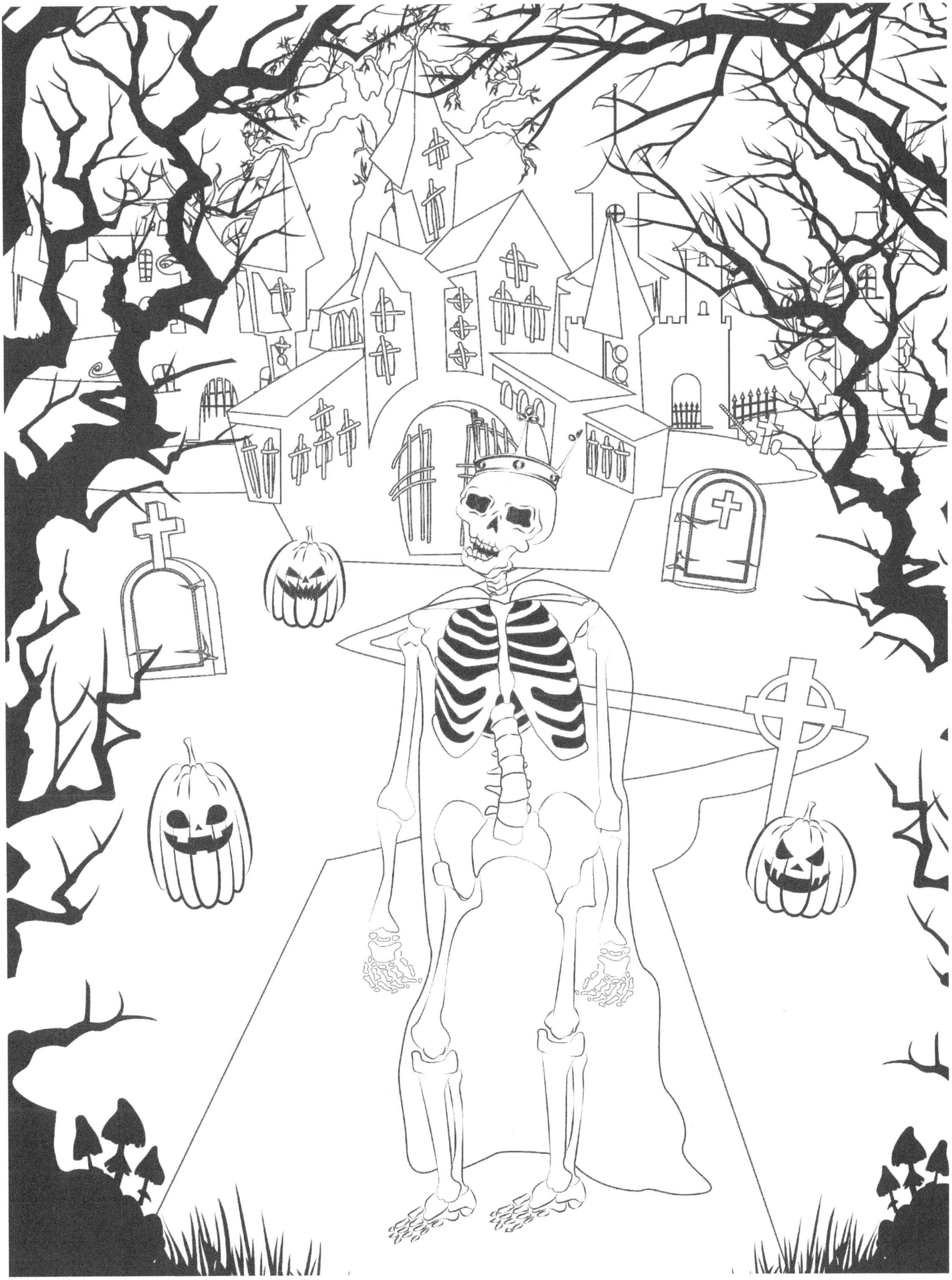

Thank you for purchasing this book.

If you would like to know more about
Aryla Publishing Books please visit:-

www.ArylaPublishing.com

Or follow us on
Facebook
Twitter
Instagram
for *free promotions*

@arylapublishing

We would love to know what you think of
this book so please leave us a review.

Have a wonderful day ☺

Other Coloring Books from Aryla Publishing

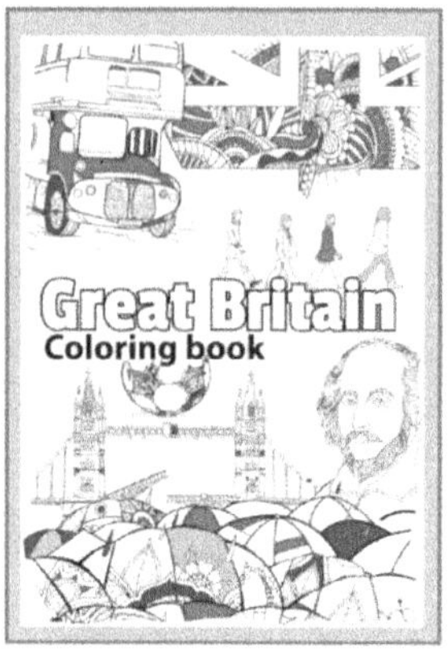

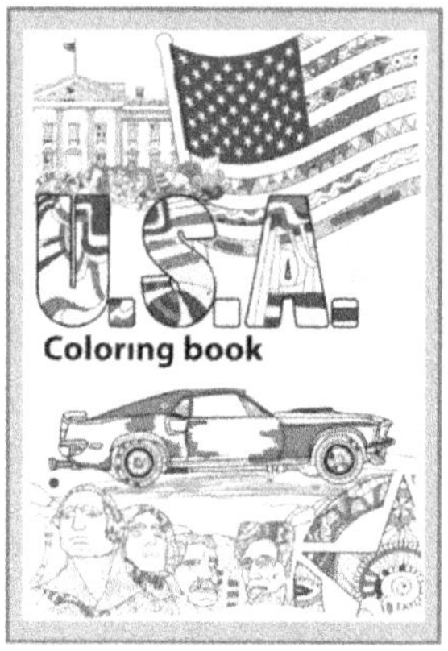

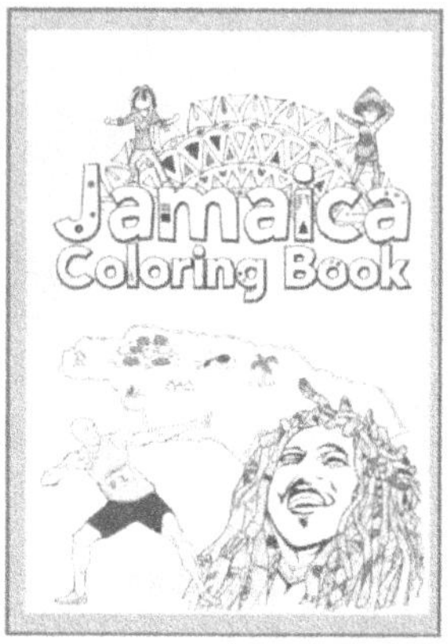

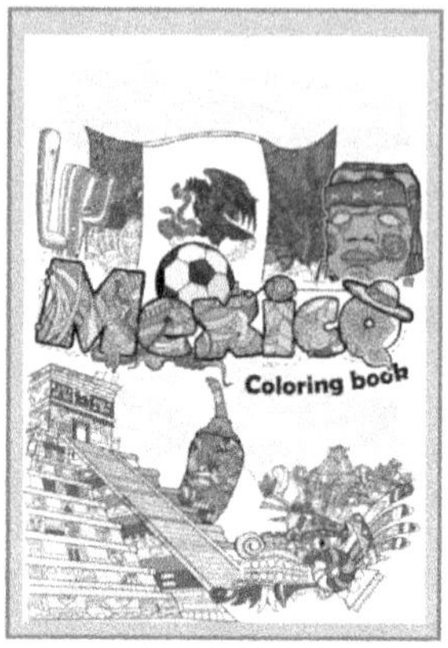

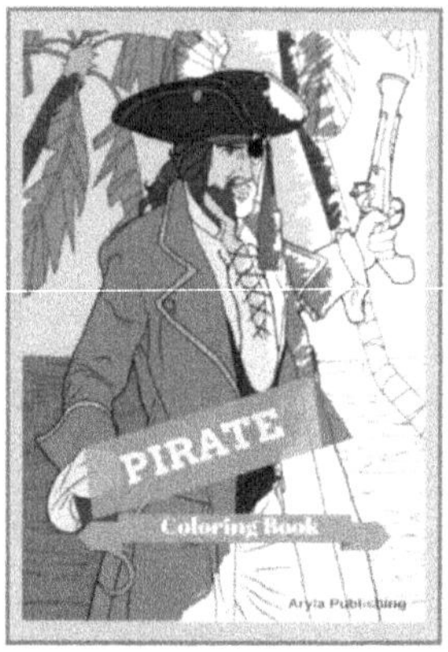

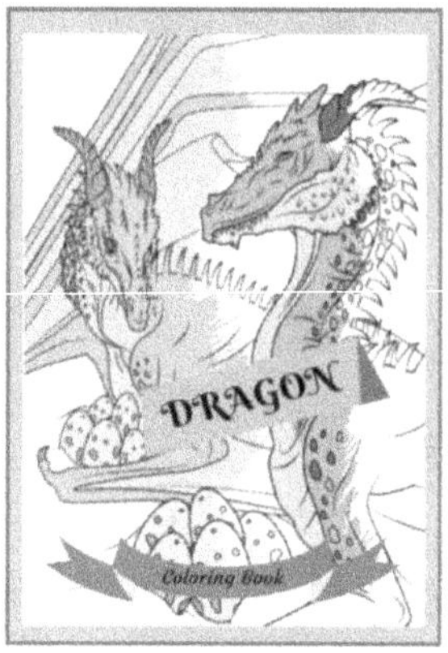

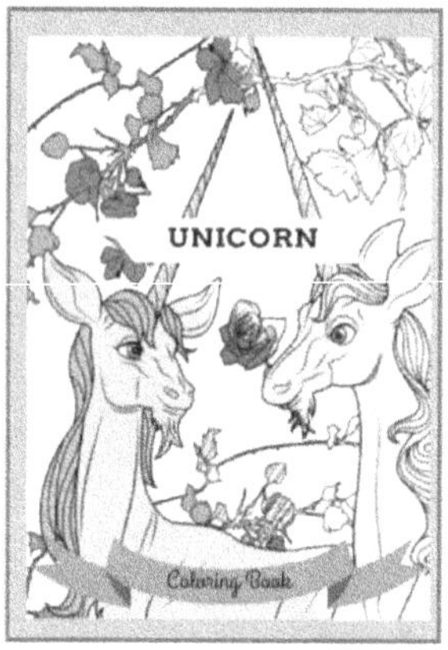

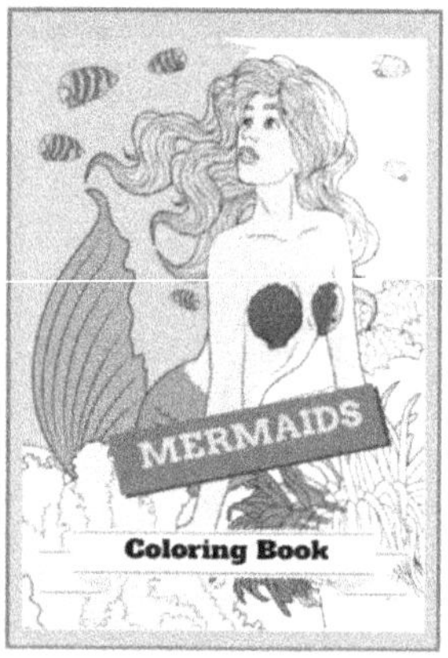

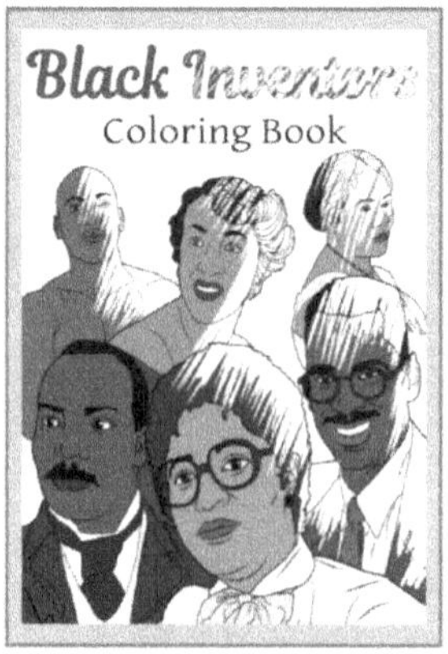

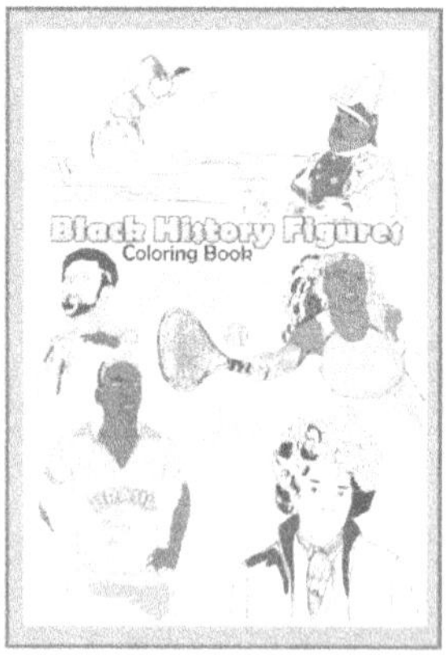

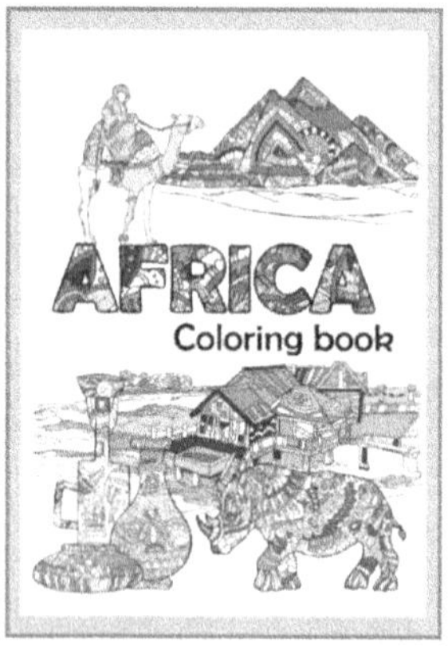

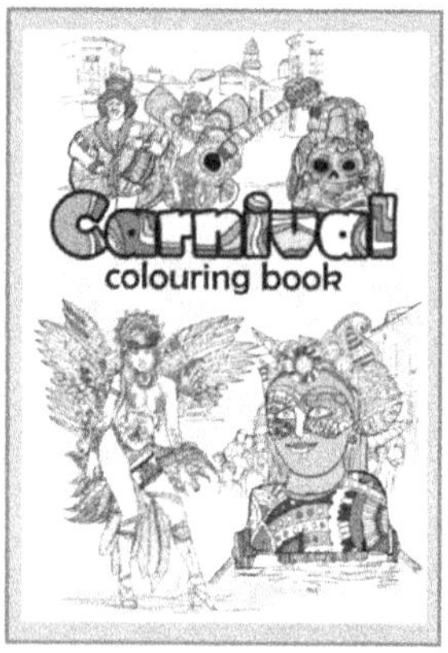

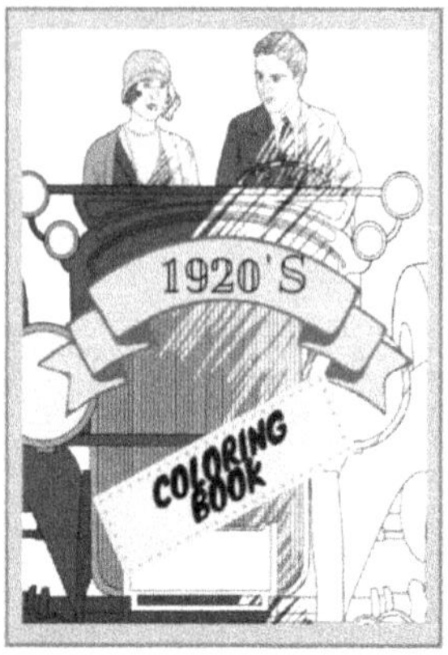

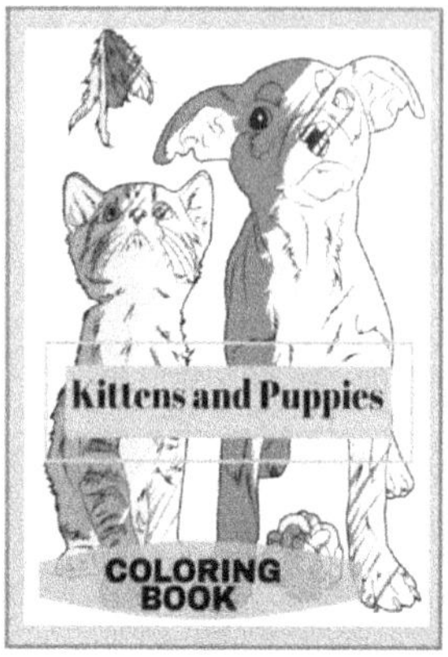

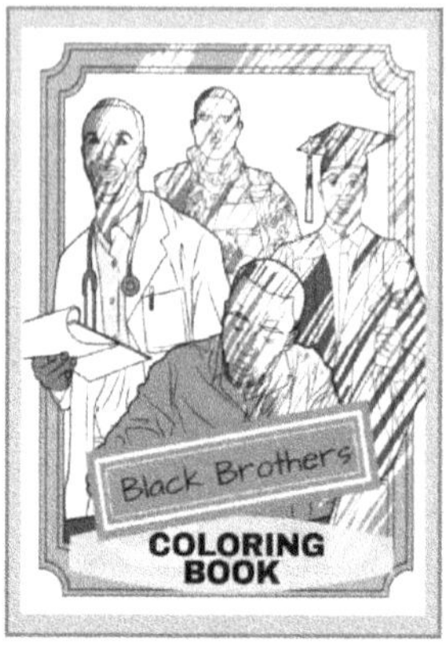

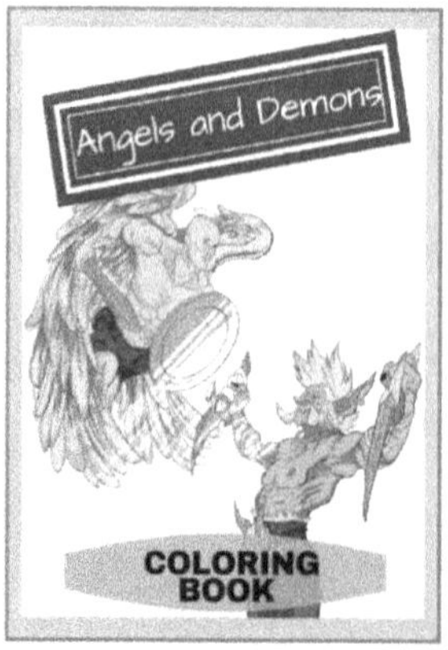

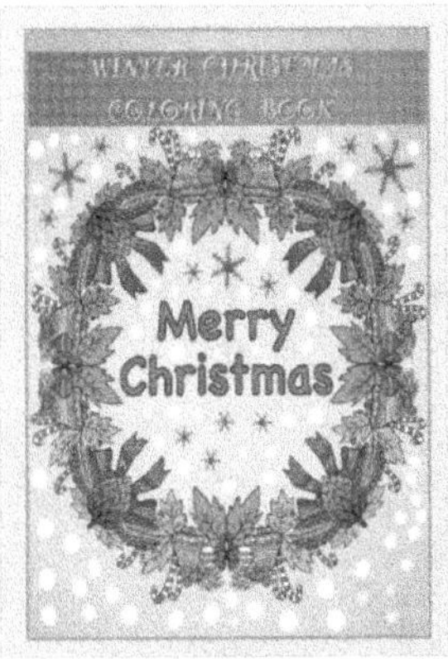
Merry
Christmas

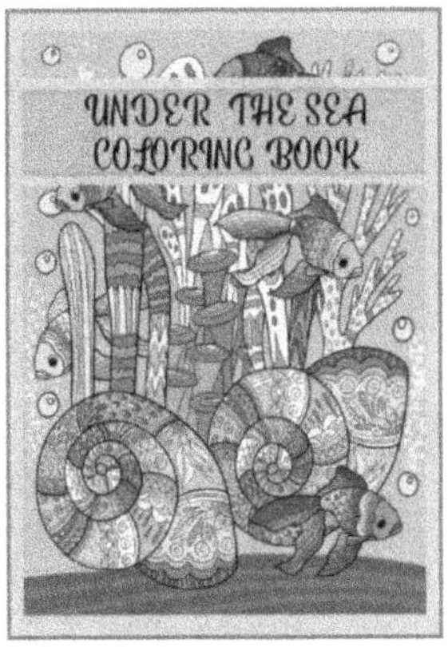
UNDER THE SEA
COLORING BOOK

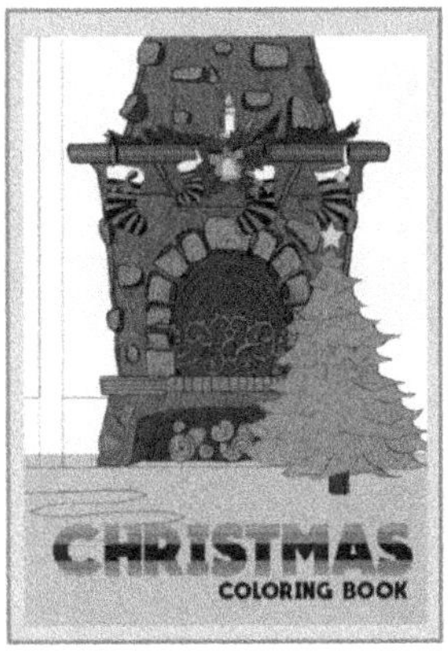
CHRISTMAS
COLORING BOOK

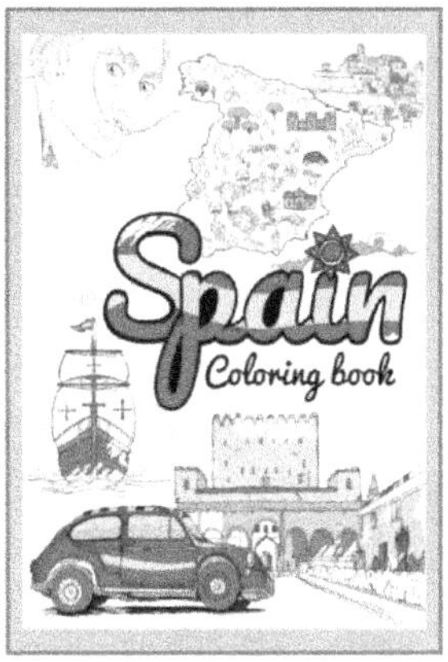
Spain
Coloring book

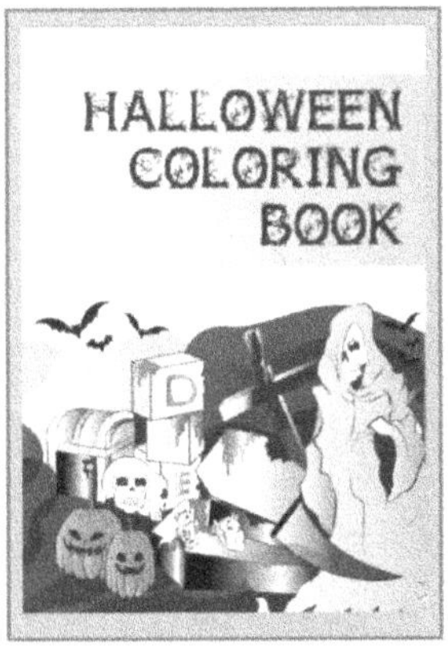
HALLOWEEN
COLORING
BOOK

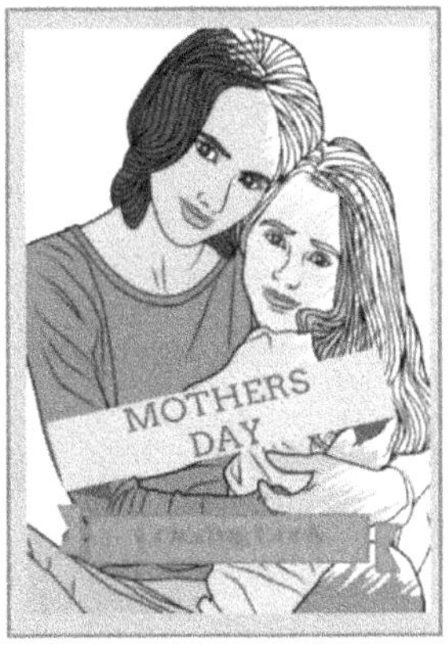
MOTHERS
DAY

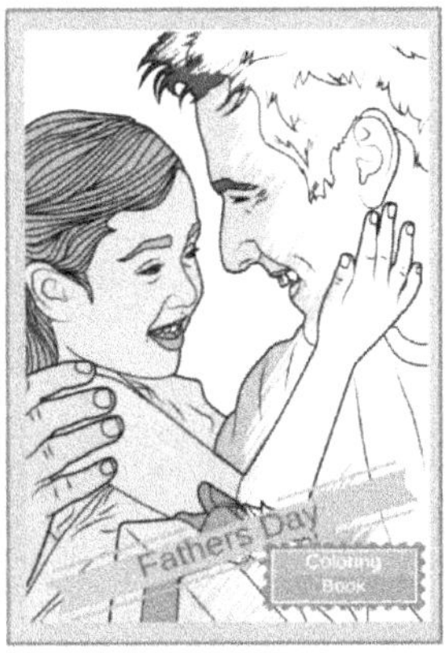
Fathers Day
Coloring
Book

HALLOWEEN 2
Coloring Book
REST IN PIECES

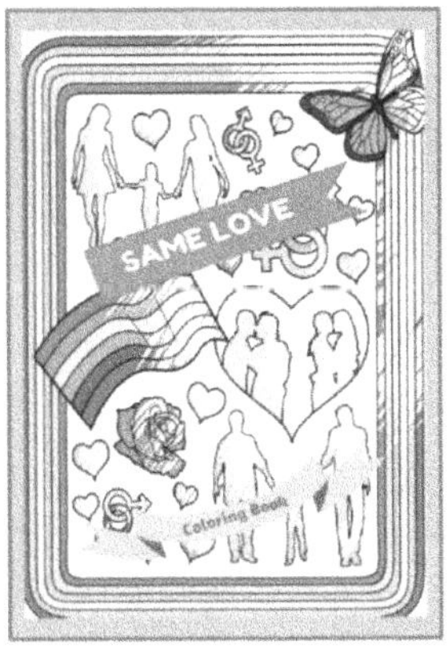
SAME LOVE
Coloring Book

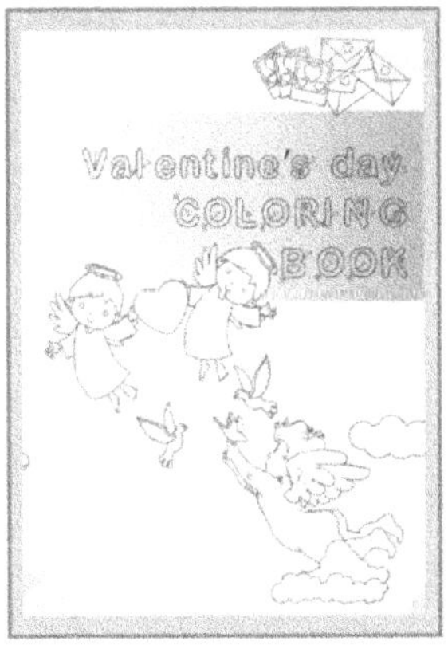
Valentine's day
COLORING
BOOK

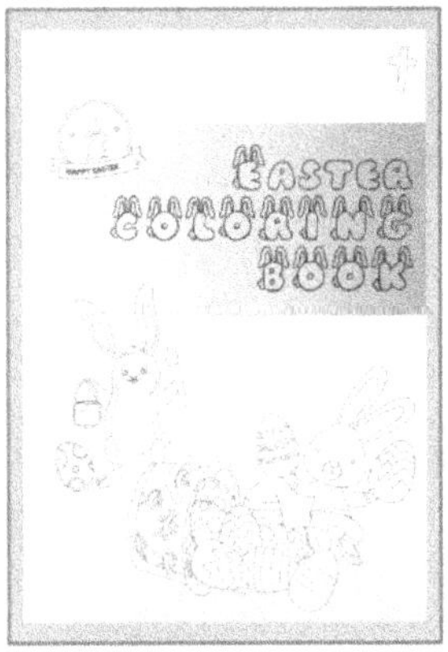
EASTER
COLORING
BOOK

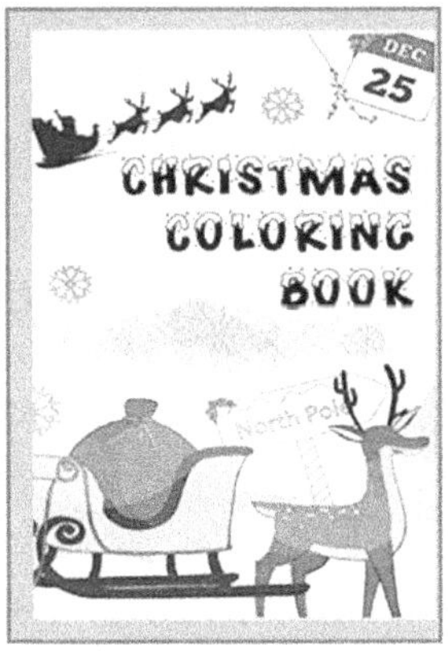
DEC
25
CHRISTMAS
COLORING
BOOK

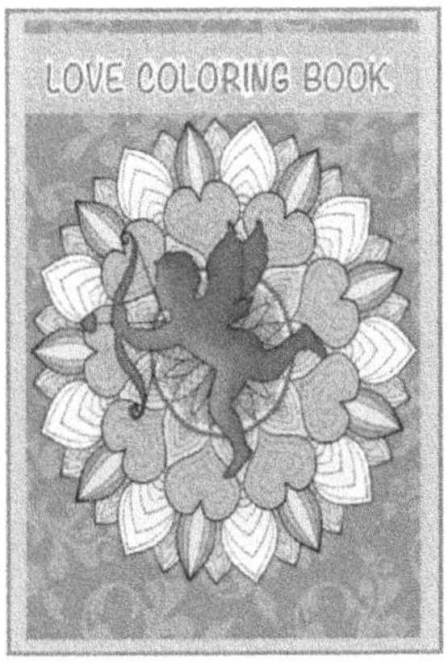
LOVE COLORING BOOK

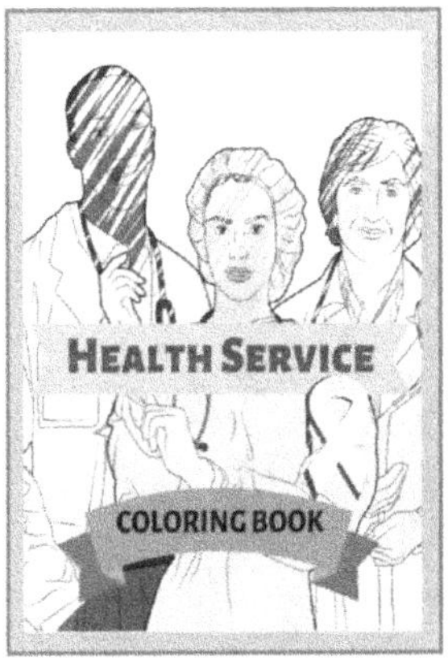
HEALTH SERVICE
COLORING BOOK

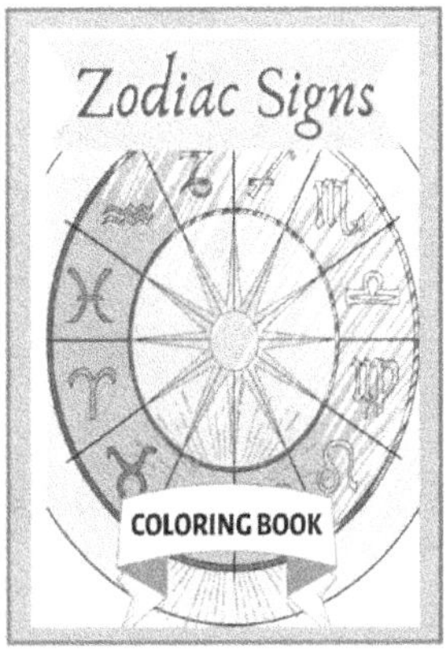
Zodiac Signs
COLORING BOOK

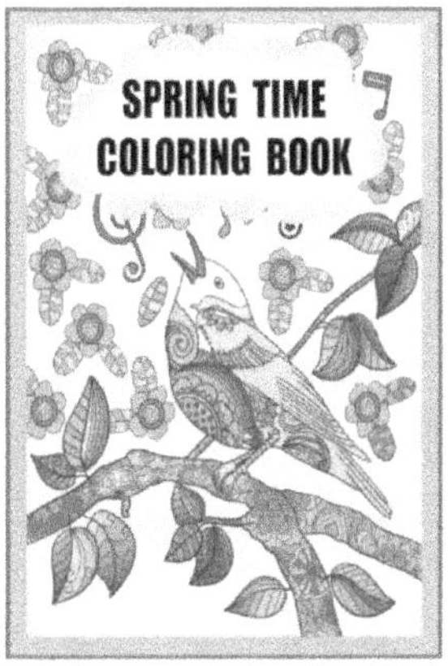
SPRING TIME
COLORING BOOK

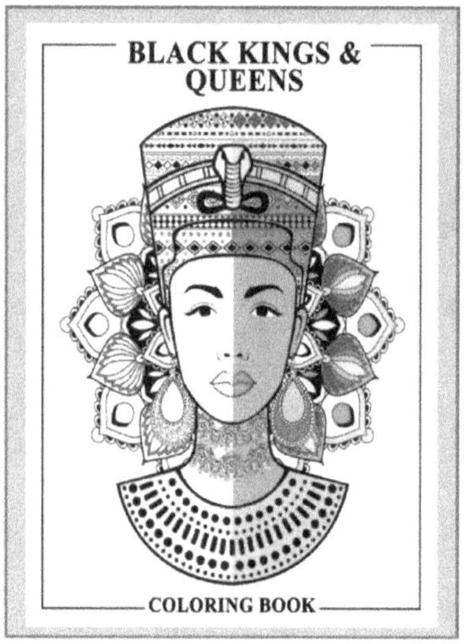
BLACK KINGS &
QUEENS
COLORING BOOK

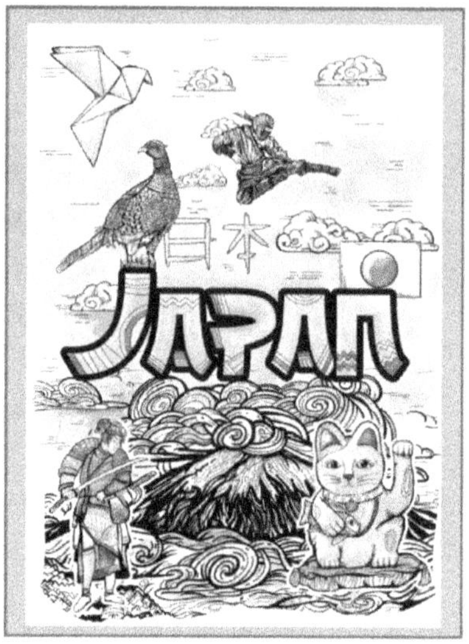
日本
JAPAN

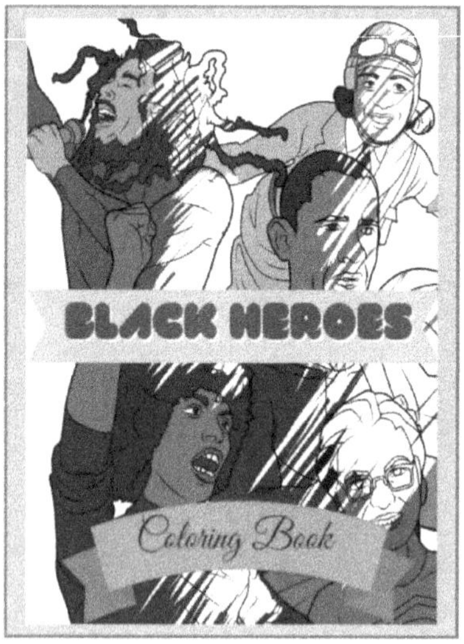
BLACK HEROES
Coloring Book

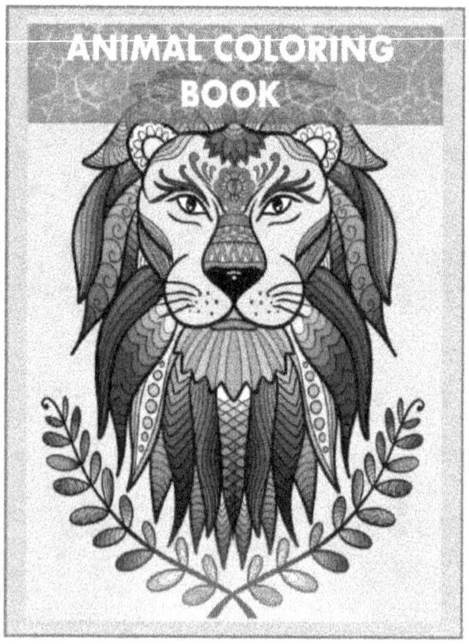
ANIMAL COLORING
BOOK

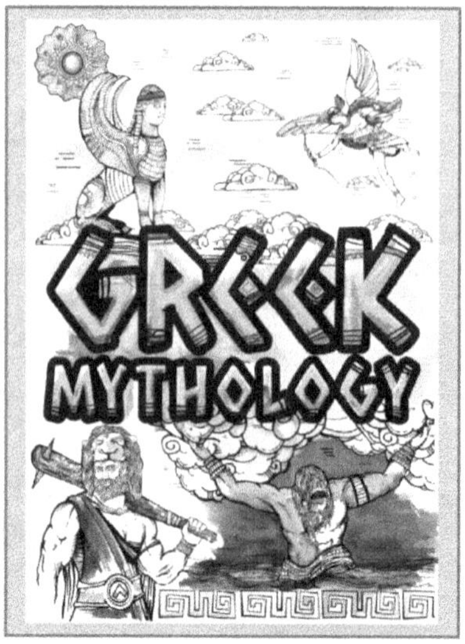
GREEK
MYTHOLOGY

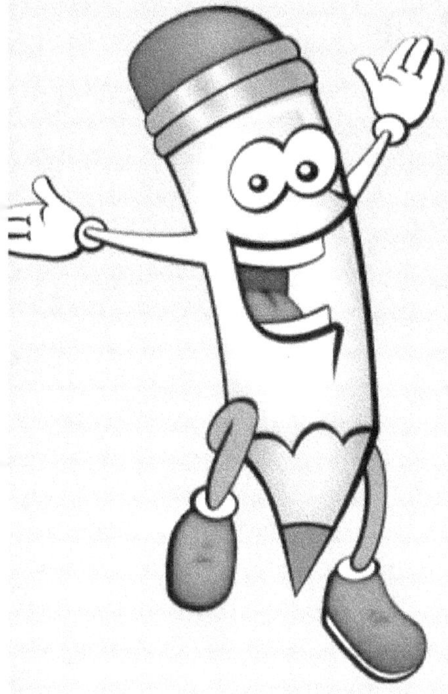

WE WOULD LOVE YOUR FEEDBACK

PLEASE LEAVE REVIEW AT:-

http://bit.ly/reviewhalloween1